AF375422

Beyond the Gut: Homoeopathy for Inflammatory Bowel Disease and Irritable Bowel Syndrome

First edition- 2024

Author

Dr. Rajneesh Kumar Sharma
BSc, BHMS, MD (Homoeopathy), DI (Hom) London,
hMD (UK), D.Lit. (UK), PhD

- Privileged/ Executive Member- Delhi Homoeopathic Medical Association
- Life Member- Homoeopathic Medical Association of India
- Life Member- Indian Institute of Homoeopathic Physicians
- Life Member- Indian Medico-legal and Ethics Association
- Medical Examiner- Life Corporation of India
- Faculty to several National and International Conferences
- Recipient of many International and National Awards
- Executive editor- Hahnemannian Homoeopathic Sandesh (A peer-reviewed journal)
- Author of numerous Research Papers, Articles, Case Presentations, and Books
- Chief Managing Director- Homoeo Cure & Research Institute, Vaibhav Homoeopathic Pharma and Sparsh Multispecialty Hospital

Dedication

In the quest against the tide of IBD's might,

We stand united, warriors in the fight.

To every soul who battles through the pain,

This book's for you, our dedication plain.

In memory of those who've gone before,

Their strength and spirit live forevermore.

And for the brave who face each dawn anew,

This verse is penned, a tribute to you.

To healthcare heroes, guiding light in dark,

Whose care and wisdom leave a lasting mark.

With every step, we journey hand in hand,

In search of healing for our fellow man.

Through homoeopathy's gentle art we find,

A path to healing, solace for the mind.

In this pursuit, our dedication's clear,

To ease the burden, banish doubt and fear.

So let this poem be a beacon bright,

A symbol of our shared resolve and might.

For in the face of IBD's cruel plight,

Together, we'll emerge into the light.

Forewords

As I reflect upon the journey chronicled within these pages, I am struck by the unwavering dedication and collective effort that have brought this book to fruition. Inflammatory Bowel Disease (IBD) and Irritable bowel syndrome (IBS) remain a formidable challenge for patients and healthcare professionals alike, demanding a comprehensive understanding and nuanced approach to treatment.

In this compendium, we embark upon a voyage through the intricate landscape of IBD and IBS, exploring its multifaceted nature and the therapeutic avenues available, particularly within the realm of homoeopathy. As a practitioner deeply committed to holistic healing, I have witnessed firsthand the profound impact that individualized homoeopathic treatment can have on patients grappling with IBD and IBS.

Homoeopathy offers a unique perspective on healthcare, viewing each patient as an integrated whole, encompassing physical, emotional, and spiritual dimensions. Through meticulous case-taking and the selection of simillimum remedies, homoeopaths aim not only to alleviate symptoms but also to address the underlying imbalances driving the disease.

Within these pages, readers will find a wealth of knowledge distilled from years of clinical experience, scholarly inquiry, and compassionate care. From the elucidation of pathophysiological mechanisms to the practical application of homoeopathic remedies, this compendium serves as a valuable resource for practitioners seeking to enhance their understanding and efficacy in managing IBD.

I extend my heartfelt appreciation to all those who have contributed to this endeavor, from the dedicated author and researchers to the patients whose journeys have inspired our work. May this book serve as a beacon of hope and healing for all those touched by IBD and IBS, guiding us toward a future where every individual can enjoy optimal health and well-being.

Dr. Amit Jain
MBBS, MS, MCh (Gasstrosurgery)
Senior Gastro-onco Consultant and HOD
Department of Gastrosurgery
Fortis Hospital, Noida

Preface

Inflammatory bowel disease (IBD) and Irritable bowel syndrome (IBS) pose a significant challenge in the realm of gastroenterology, manifesting as chronic inflammation within the gastrointestinal (GI) tract. This complex condition encompasses a spectrum of disorders, prominently featuring Crohn's disease and ulcerative colitis (UC), both of which entail relapsing and remitting inflammation patterns affecting various segments of the colon and small intestine. Symptoms such as diarrhea and abdominal pain underscore the chronic nature of these inflammatory conditions.

Despite significant advancements in medical science, the etiology of IBD and Irritable bowel syndrome (IBS) remains elusive. However, emerging research suggests multifactorial contributions, implicating both genetic predispositions and environmental triggers. Factors such as saccharin ingestion have been proposed as potential culprits, exerting deleterious effects on gut microbiota and mucosal integrity, thereby predisposing individuals to inflammatory responses.

The pathophysiology of IBD and Irritable bowel syndrome (IBS) involves intricate immune dysregulation, wherein aberrant immune reactions in the GI mucosa lead to the release of inflammatory mediators, perpetuating chronic inflammation. The interplay between genetic susceptibility and environmental triggers further complicates the disease process, highlighting the need for a comprehensive understanding of its underlying mechanisms.

Classification of IBD encompasses various types, ranging from well-defined entities such as Crohn's disease and UC to unclassified presentations that defy conventional categorization. Each subtype exhibits distinct clinical features and pathological characteristics, necessitating tailored approaches to diagnosis and management.

In this comprehensive guide, we delve into the intricacies of IBD and IBS, exploring their diverse manifestations and diagnostic modalities. From gastrointestinal symptoms to extra-intestinal manifestations, we aim to provide clinicians and researchers with a holistic perspective on this challenging condition.

Furthermore, we emphasize the potential of homoeopathic interventions in managing IBD and IBS, offering unique advantages over conventional treatments. Homoeopathy, with its individualized approach and focus on addressing underlying imbalances, presents a promising alternative for patients seeking holistic and personalized care. By harnessing the body's innate healing mechanisms, homoeopathic remedies aim to alleviate symptoms, restore balance, and promote long-term well-being. Drawing upon the latest research and clinical insights, this preface sets the stage for a deeper exploration of IBD and IBS and its multifaceted dimensions. We hope that this compendium serves as a valuable resource for healthcare professionals navigating the complexities of IBD and IBS, ultimately enhancing patient care and outcomes in this evolving field of gastroenterology.

Dr. Rajneesh Kumar Sharma

Contents

Abstract

The relapsing and remitting (Psora) inflammatory conditions of the GI tract, including Crohn's disease and ulcerative colitis (UC), are collectively called as Inflammatory bowel disease (IBD), characterized by chronic inflammation (Psora/ Sycosis/ Syphilis) at various sites in the colon and small intestine, resulting in diarrhea and abdominal pain.

The cause of IBD is still unknown. Saccharin may be a key causative factor for IBD, through its inhibition of gut bacteria and the resultant impaired inactivation of digestive proteases and over-digestion of the mucus layer and gut barrier. (Causa occasionalis)

It is seen that a cell-mediated immune response in the GI mucosa leads to inflammation by release of inflammatory mediators, including cytokines, interleukins, and tissue necrotic factor (TNF) (Psora). The normal intestinal flora triggers an abnormal immune reaction in individuals with a multifactorial genetic tendency (Syphilis). These factors possibly involve abnormal epithelial barriers and mucosal immune defense mechanisms (Psora). Crohn's disease and ulcerative colitis, are both caused by a weakening in gut barrier (Psora/ Syphilis) and only differ in that UC is mainly due to increased infiltration of gut bacteria and the resultant recruitment of neutrophils and formation of crypt abscess (Psora/ Syphilis), while CD is mainly due to increased infiltration of antigens and particles from gut lumen and the resultant recruitment of macrophages and formation of granulomas (Psora/ Sycosis).

Classification of inflammatory bowel disease (IBD) encompasses various types, including a category known as "unclassified." In some instances, cases do not fit neatly into predefined categories and are thus labeled as unclassified. Additionally, when a surgical pathology specimen cannot be definitively classified, it is referred to as indeterminate colitis.

Irritable Bowel Syndrome (IBS) is a functional gastrointestinal disorder characterized by abdominal pain, bloating, and changes in bowel habits without evidence of structural or biochemical abnormalities.

Irritable Bowel Syndrome (IBS) is a complex gastrointestinal disorder characterized by various symptoms, including abdominal pain, bloating, and changes in bowel habits. While the exact cause of IBS remains unclear, several factors have been implicated in its development. Abnormal gastrointestinal motility, hypersensitivity to pain and discomfort, and food sensitivities are among the potential contributors. Stress and psychological factors, such as anxiety and depression, can exacerbate symptoms or trigger flare-ups. Imbalances in the gut microbiota, alterations in the gut-brain axis, and genetic predispositions may also play a role. Additionally, inflammation, albeit low-grade, and disruptions in serotonin levels have been associated with IBS. Other factors, including hormonal changes, infections, and prior gastrointestinal illnesses, further contribute to the complexity of IBS and its diverse symptomatology.

Homoeopathy, with its emphasis on individualized treatment and holistic healing, offers a compelling framework for addressing the multifaceted nature of IBD. Through careful case analysis and the selection of tailored remedies, homoeopaths endeavor to not only alleviate symptoms but also to address the underlying imbalances driving disease.

Keywords

IBS, Irritable bowel syndrome, IBD, Inflammatory bowel doisease, Ulcerative colitis, Crohn's disease

Part- one

Inflammatory Bowel Disease

Historical Review of Inflammatory Bowel Disease

The timeline of discovery and evolution of research in Inflammatory Bowel Disease (IBD) spans over several centuries, marked by significant milestones and breakthroughs that have shaped our understanding and management of these complex conditions.

19th Century

1833: Sir Thomas Addison describes "chronic idiopathic ulceration of the mucous membrane of the colon and rectum" later recognized as ulcerative colitis.

1859: Samuel Wilks and Sir Arthur Rutherford Morison publish seminal works on ulcerative colitis, laying the foundation for its clinical characterization.

1885: Giovanni Battista Morgagni introduces the term "Crohn's disease" in his work on regional enteritis.

20th Century

1920s-1930s: The association between smoking and ulcerative colitis is recognized, with observations suggesting a protective effect.

1950s-1960s: Landmark studies by Burrill B. Crohn, Leon Ginzburg, and Gordon D. Oppenheimer delineate the clinical features and pathology of Crohn's disease, distinct from ulcerative colitis.

1960s-1970s: Advances in endoscopy and histopathology facilitate the differentiation between Crohn's disease and ulcerative colitis, refining diagnostic criteria.

1970s-1980s: The introduction of corticosteroids revolutionizes the management of IBD, offering effective control of acute flares and inflammation.

1980s-1990s: Immunomodulators such as azathioprine and 6-mercaptopurine emerge as important therapeutic options for maintenance therapy in IBD.

1990s-2000s: The advent of biologic agents targeting tumor necrosis factor-alpha (TNF-a), such as infliximab and adalimumab, revolutionizes the treatment landscape for IBD, offering new avenues for achieving remission and mucosal healing.

2000s-Present

The era of personalized medicine dawns, with advances in genetics and molecular biology shedding light on the intricate interplay between host genetics, environmental factors, and the gut microbiome in the pathogenesis of IBD.

Precision medicine approaches, including pharmacogenomics and microbiota-targeted therapies, hold promise for tailored and more effective management strategies.

Throughout this timeline, collaborative efforts between clinicians, researchers, and patients have been instrumental in driving progress in IBD research, from elucidating underlying mechanisms to developing novel therapeutics and refining diagnostic techniques. As we stand on the cusp of a new era in IBD management, characterized by personalized and targeted approaches, the journey of discovery and innovation continues, fueled by a shared commitment to improving outcomes and quality of life for individuals living with these chronic inflammatory conditions.

Definition of Inflammatory Bowel Disease

The relapsing and remitting inflammatory conditions affecting the gastrointestinal (GI) tract, encompassing ailments such as Crohn's disease and ulcerative colitis (UC), collectively fall under the umbrella term of Inflammatory Bowel Disease (IBD). These conditions are marked by chronic inflammation occurring at multiple sites within the colon and small intestine, leading to distressing symptoms including diarrhea and abdominal pain.

Inflammatory Bowel Disease (IBD) profoundly impacts the lives of millions worldwide. At the heart of IBD lies a perplexing interplay of immune dysregulation and environmental triggers, culminating in a diverse array of symptoms and clinical presentations.

Among the constellation of disorders that comprise IBD, Crohn's disease and ulcerative colitis (UC) stand out as primary protagonists, each with its own unique pathophysiological footprint. Crohn's disease, characterized by transmural inflammation that can affect any part of the GI tract from mouth to anus, manifests with a penchant for segmental involvement and the potential for complications such as strictures, fistulas, and abscesses. On the other hand, UC predominantly targets the colon and rectum, precipitating continuous mucosal inflammation that gives rise to symptoms like bloody diarrhea, urgency, and tenesmus.

The hallmark of IBD lies in its relapsing and remitting nature, with patients experiencing periods of exacerbation interspersed with intervals of relative quiescence. This fluctuating disease course not only imparts a profound physical toll but also exacts a heavy emotional burden on those affected, impacting various facets of daily life and wellbeing.

Central to the management of IBD is a multifaceted approach that addresses both the acute symptoms and the underlying inflammatory processes driving disease progression. From conventional pharmacotherapy aimed at inducing and maintaining remission to surgical interventions reserved for refractory cases or complications, the armamentarium against IBD is vast and evolving.

Yet, amidst the myriad therapeutic modalities, one modality stands out for its unique approach to healing – homoeopathy. Grounded in the principles of individualization and similia similibus curentur (let like be cured by like), homoeopathy offers a holistic framework for managing IBD that seeks to rebalance the body's vital force and restore harmony to disrupted physiological processes. By tailoring remedies to each patient's unique symptomatology and constitutional makeup, homoeopaths aim to not only alleviate acute symptoms but also address the underlying imbalances that predispose individuals to IBD.

In the pages that follow, we delve into the intricacies of IBD, exploring its etiology, pathogenesis, clinical manifestations, and management strategies from the dual perspectives of conventional medicine and homoeopathy. It is our sincere hope that this compendium will serve as a beacon of knowledge and empowerment for healthcare professionals and patients alike, fostering collaboration and understanding in the ongoing battle against IBD.

Pathophysiology of Inflammatory Bowel Disease

The exact underlying causes of inflammatory bowel disease (IBD), including Crohn's disease and ulcerative colitis (UC), remain elusive. However, research suggests that a complex interplay of factors contributes to the development of these conditions.

One prominent factor is a dysregulated immune response within the gastrointestinal (GI) mucosa, characterized by the release of inflammatory mediators such as cytokines, interleukins, and tissue necrotic factor (TNF). This cell-mediated immune response, often associated with Psora, triggers chronic inflammation, a hallmark feature of IBD.

Another contributing factor is believed to be a multifactorial genetic predisposition combined with environmental triggers. Individuals with a genetic tendency may experience an abnormal immune reaction initiated by the normal intestinal flora. This immune dysregulation, reminiscent of Syphilis, sets the stage for chronic inflammation and tissue damage within the GI tract.

Central to the pathogenesis of IBD is the compromise of epithelial barriers and mucosal immune defense mechanisms, factors often associated with Psora. The weakening of these protective barriers allows for the infiltration of antigens, particles, and gut bacteria into the intestinal mucosa, triggering an inflammatory cascade.

In Crohn's disease, this inflammatory process primarily manifests as increased infiltration of antigens and particles from the gut lumen, leading to the recruitment of macrophages and the formation of granulomas. This pattern of inflammation, reflective of both Psora and Sycosis, contributes to the characteristic transmural inflammation and skip lesions observed in Crohn's disease.

On the other hand, in ulcerative colitis, the predominant mechanism involves increased infiltration of gut bacteria, leading to the recruitment of neutrophils and the formation of crypt abscesses. This localized inflammation, also influenced by Psora and Syphilis, primarily affects the mucosal layer of the colon, resulting in continuous inflammation and ulceration.

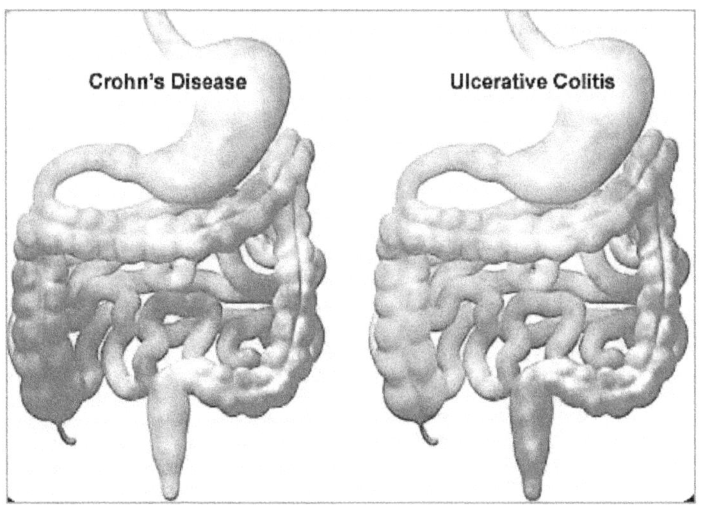

Overall, the pathogenesis of IBD is multifaceted, involving a complex interplay of immune dysregulation, genetic predisposition, and environmental factors. Understanding these intricate mechanisms is crucial for developing targeted therapies and improving the management of these debilitating conditions.

No specific environmental, dietary, or infectious causes are still known that trigger this reaction. However, the following factors modify IBD-

- Appendectomy appears to lower the risk of ulcerative colitis
- Cigarette smoking helps in the development or exacerbation of Crohn's disease but decreases the risk of ulcerative colitis
- It is seen that people with higher socioeconomic status are likely to have Crohn's disease
- NSAIDs may exacerbate IBD
- Oral contraceptives may increase the risk of Crohn's disease
- Perinatal illness and the use of antibiotics in childhood may cause increased risk of IBD

Etiology of Inflammatory Bowel Disease

The exact etiology of inflammatory bowel disease (IBD) remains a subject of ongoing research and debate within the medical community. While the precise cause is yet to be definitively determined, emerging evidence suggests that certain environmental factors, including dietary components, may play a role in the development and exacerbation of IBD.

One such potential factor is saccharin, a commonly used artificial sweetener found in various food and beverage products. Recent studies have proposed that saccharin could act as a key causative factor for IBD by disrupting the delicate balance of gut microbiota.

Saccharin's inhibitory effects on gut bacteria may lead to dysbiosis, an imbalance in the microbial composition of the intestines. This dysbiosis can have far-reaching consequences for gut health.

One proposed mechanism involves the impaired inactivation of digestive proteases due to dysbiosis induced by saccharin. Proteases are enzymes which are responsible for break down of proteins during digestion. When these proteases are not adequately inactivated, there is a risk of over-digestion of the protective mucus layer that lines the intestinal epithelium.

The mucus layer serves as a crucial barrier that protects the underlying intestinal epithelial cells from the harsh luminal environment and potential pathogens. Disruption of this mucus layer, caused by over-digestion, can compromise the integrity of the gut barrier, leading to increased permeability and susceptibility to inflammation.

Furthermore, saccharin-induced dysbiosis may exacerbate inflammation within the gut mucosa, contributing to the pathogenesis of IBD. The altered microbial composition may trigger an abnormal immune response, further fueling the chronic inflammatory process characteristic of IBD.

While these findings provide intriguing insights into a potential link between saccharin consumption and IBD, further research is needed to fully elucidate the underlying mechanisms and establish causality definitively. Nonetheless, these discoveries underscore the importance of dietary factors in modulating gut health and highlight the need for continued investigation into the role of environmental triggers in IBD pathogenesis.

Types of Inflammatory Bowel Disease

Unclassified

The classification of inflammatory bowel disease (IBD) is a complex endeavor, encompassing various types and subtypes that reflect the diverse clinical presentations and underlying pathophysiology of the condition. Among these classifications, there exists a category known as "unclassified," which denotes cases that do not fit neatly into predefined diagnostic criteria or fail to exhibit the distinct features characteristic of Crohn's disease or ulcerative colitis.

Unclassified IBD poses a diagnostic challenge for clinicians, as these cases often present with atypical clinical manifestations or ambiguous histopathological findings. In such instances, healthcare providers may encounter difficulty in accurately categorizing the condition based on conventional criteria, leading to the designation of unclassified IBD.

One particular scenario where unclassified IBD may arise is when a surgical pathology specimen fails to exhibit the characteristic features of either Crohn's disease or ulcerative colitis. In such cases, the histopathological evaluation may reveal inconclusive findings or overlapping features that do not align with the diagnostic criteria for either subtype of IBD. Consequently, the condition is labeled as indeterminate colitis, signifying the uncertainty surrounding its classification.

Unclassified IBD underscores the heterogeneous nature of the disease and highlights the limitations of current diagnostic approaches in capturing its full spectrum. As our understanding of IBD continues to evolve and diagnostic techniques advance, efforts are underway to refine classification criteria and improve diagnostic accuracy, thereby facilitating more personalized and targeted approaches to patient care.

Classified

1. Crohn's Disease:

- **Location:** Predominantly affects the small bowel, but can involve any part of the digestive tract from mouth to anus.
- **Recto-Sigmoid Involvement:** Often spared, distinguishing it from ulcerative colitis.
- **Colonic Involvement:** Typically, right-sided, with transmural inflammation.
- **Symptoms:** Variable, including abdominal pain, diarrhea, weight loss, and fatigue.
- **Complications:** Fistulas, strictures, abscesses, and perianal disease are common.
- **Endoscopic Findings:** Patchy inflammation with skip lesions, cobblestone appearance, and deep ulcers.
- **Histology:** Transmural inflammation, granulomas (in some cases), and fissures.
- **Treatment:** Depends on disease severity and location, may include medication, surgery, or both.

2. Ulcerative Colitis (UC):

- **Location:** Limited to the colon and rectum.
- **Recto-Sigmoid Involvement:** Invariably involved, distinguishing it from Crohn's disease.
- **Colonic Involvement:** Typically left-sided, with continuous mucosal inflammation.
- **Symptoms:** Bloody diarrhea, abdominal pain, urgency, and tenesmus.
- **Complications:** Fulminant colitis, toxic megacolon, and colorectal cancer.
- **Endoscopic Findings:** Continuous mucosal inflammation starting from the rectum.
- **Histology:** Mucosal inflammation, crypt abscesses, and distortion of crypt architecture.
- **Treatment:** Medications such as aminosalicylates, corticosteroids, immunomodulators, and biologics, along with surgery in severe cases.

3. Indeterminate Colitis:

- **Definition:** Represents cases that do not fit the criteria for either Crohn's disease or ulcerative colitis.
- **Diagnostic Challenge:** Due to ambiguous clinical, endoscopic, or histological findings.
- **Management:** Treatment approach similar to Crohn's disease or UC, depending on the clinical course and severity of symptoms.

4. Other Classified IBDs:

- **Microscopic Colitis:** Characterized by chronic, nonbloody diarrhea and normal colonoscopy with abnormal histology.
- **Collagenous Colitis:** Subtype of microscopic colitis characterized by a thickened subepithelial collagen band.
- **Lymphocytic Colitis:** Subtype of microscopic colitis characterized by increased intraepithelial lymphocytes.
- **Behçet's Disease:** Multisystem inflammatory disorder involving recurrent oral and genital ulcers, skin lesions, and eye inflammation.
- **Primary Sclerosing Cholangitis (PSC):** Chronic progressive inflammatory disease affecting the bile ducts, often associated with UC.

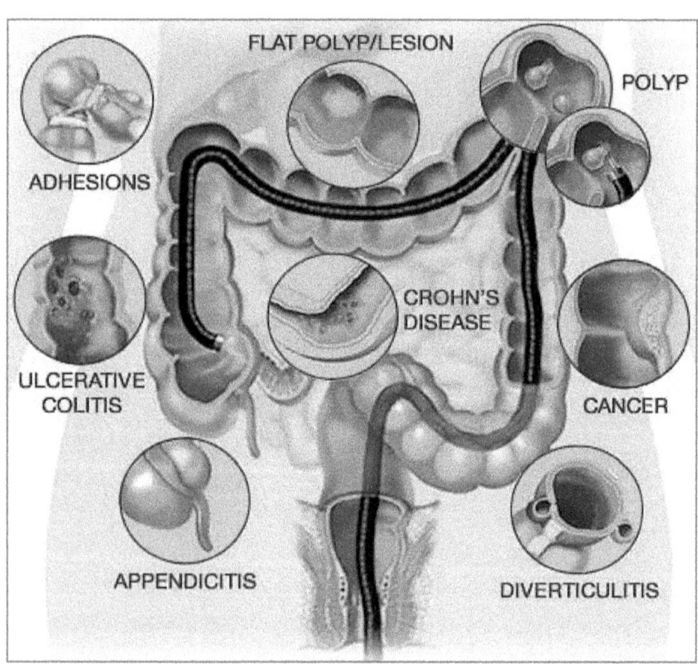

Overall Approach:

- Accurate diagnosis crucial for appropriate management.
- Multidisciplinary approach involving gastroenterologists, pathologists, radiologists, and surgeons.
- Treatment aims to induce and maintain remission, prevent complications, and improve quality of life.

Signs and symptoms of Inflammatory Bowel Disease

Inflammatory bowel disease has following signs and symptoms in general-

1. Diarrhea:

- Frequent, urgent bowel movements.
- Loose or watery stools, sometimes with blood or mucus.

2. Abdominal Pain:

- Cramping or sharp pain in the abdomen, often in the lower right or lower left quadrant.
- May vary in intensity and duration.

3. Rectal Bleeding:

- Blood in the stool, ranging from bright red to dark maroon.
- Blood may be visible on toilet paper or in the toilet bowl.

4. Weight Loss:

- Unintentional weight loss due to poor nutrient absorption, reduced appetite, or chronic inflammation.

5. Fatigue:

- Persistent tiredness, weakness, or lack of energy.

- May be exacerbated by anemia or disrupted sleep patterns.

6. Fever:

- Low-grade fever or persistent elevated temperature.
- Often accompanies active disease flare-ups.

7. Abdominal Cramps:

- Spasmodic abdominal discomfort or cramping.
- May worsen after eating or during bowel movements.

8. Malnutrition:

- Inadequate absorption of nutrients due to inflammation or malabsorption.
- Can lead to deficiencies in vitamins, minerals, and protein.

9. Perianal Symptoms:

- Pain, itching, or irritation around the anus.
- Anal fissures, fistulas, or abscesses may develop.

10. Extraintestinal Manifestations:

- Joint pain or swelling (arthritis).
- Skin rashes, ulcers, or lesions (dermatitis).
- Eye inflammation (uveitis or iritis).
- Mouth sores or ulcers (oral aphthous ulcers).

11. Bowel Obstruction:

- Partial or complete blockage of the intestines.
- Causes severe abdominal pain, nausea, vomiting, and constipation.

12. Delayed Growth and Development:

- Particularly in children and adolescents with IBD.
- Due to malnutrition, medication side effects, or chronic inflammation.

13. Changes in Bowel Habits:

- Alternating between periods of constipation and diarrhea.
- Irregularity in bowel movements, urgency, or incomplete evacuation.

14. Psychological Symptoms:

- Anxiety, depression, or mood swings.
- Often related to the chronic nature of the disease and its impact on daily life.

15. Reduced Quality of Life:

- Impaired social functioning, work productivity, and overall well-being.
- May result from the physical symptoms, psychological distress, and lifestyle adjustments associated with IBD.

Gastrointestinal Symptoms

Chronic abdominal pain accompanied by persistent bloody or non-bloody diarrhea lasting more than four weeks is indicative of inflammatory bowel disease (IBD). Additional associated features include: -

- **Anemia:** Often due to chronic inflammation and poor nutrient absorption.
- **Evidence of Inflammation:** Elevated C-reactive protein (CRP) and platelets are common markers.
- **Family History of IBD:** Genetic predisposition may play a role.
- **Nocturnal Diarrhea:** Diarrheal episodes occurring at night, suggestive of more severe disease.
- **Nutritional Deficiencies:** Such as iron, B12, folate, and low albumin levels due to malabsorption.
- **Weight Loss:** Resulting from reduced appetite, malnutrition, or chronic inflammation.

Extra-intestinal Manifestations

Both Crohn's disease and Ulcerative colitis both affect the person as a whole i.e. various parts of the body beyond the gastrointestinal tract. Most extra-intestinal manifestations are more common in ulcerative colitis than in Crohn disease, as it is limited to the small bowel. Extra-intestinal manifestations of inflammatory bowel disease may be grouped into three categories: -

Parallel disorders

These include-

- **Aphthous stomatitis-** Aphthous stomatitis, or canker sores, are painful ulcers that form inside the mouth, often triggered by stress or minor mouth injuries. (Psora/ Syphilis)
- **Episcleritis-** Episcleritis is inflammation of the episclera, causing redness and irritation but typically does not affecting the vision (Psora/ Sycosis)
- **Erythema nodosum-** a skin condition characterized by painful, red nodules or lumps that develop under the skin, usually on the shins. It can be associated with various underlying conditions such as infections, autoimmune diseases, medications, or inflammatory bowel disease. (Psora/ Sycosis)
- **Peripheral arthritis-** inflammation of the joints in the arms and legs, excluding the spine. It can cause pain, swelling, stiffness, and decreased mobility in the affected joints. This type of arthritis is common in conditions like rheumatoid arthritis, psoriatic arthritis, and reactive arthritis. (Psora/ Sycosis)
- **Pyoderma gangrenosum-** a rare skin condition characterized by painful ulcers or sores typically startimg as small, red bumps that rapidly progress into larger, deep ulcers with undermined borders. Pyoderma gangrenosum is often associated with underlying systemic diseases such as inflammatory bowel disease, rheumatoid

arthritis, or blood disorders. (Psora/ Sycosis/ Syphilis)

Concomitant disorders

Disorders that often coexist with IBD include: -

- **Ankylosing spondylitis-** in association with HLA-B27 (Psora/ Sycosis/ Syphilis)
- **Primary sclerosing cholangitis-** before IBD or parallel (Psora/ Sycosis/ Syphilis)
- **Sacroiliitis-** inflammation of the sacroiliac joints, commonly associated with conditions like ankylosing spondylitis, psoriatic arthritis, or inflammatory bowel disease. (Psora/ Syphilis)
- **Uveitis**- inflammation of the uvea, causing eye pain, redness, and blurred vision. (Psora/ Syphilis)
- **Liver disease-** fatty liver, autoimmune hepatitis, pericholangitis, cirrhosis (Psora/ Sycosis/ Syphilis)

Subsequent disorders

Complications that may arise as a result of severe Crohn's disease include: -

- **Malabsorption-** may result from extensive ileal resection (Psora/ Syphilis)
- **Kidney stones-** from excessive dietary oxalate absorption (Psora)
- **Hydroureter and hydronephrosis-** due to ureteral compression by the intestinal inflammatory process (Psora/ Sycosis)
- **Gallstones-** from impaired ileal reabsorption of bile salts (Psora)

- **Amyloidosis-** secondary to long-standing inflammatory and suppurative disease (Psora/ Sycosis/ Syphilis)

Thromboembolic Disease: Individuals with IBD are at increased risk of thromboembolic events due to various factors associated with the disease.

Crohn's disease

There are four major manifestations of Crohn's disease-

Inflammation

- Abdominal pain localized over inflamed areas (Psora)
- Diarrhea, occasional fever, weight loss (Psora/ Syphilis)
- Obstructive symptoms secondary to inflammation (Psora/ Sycosis)
- Toxic megacolon (Psora/ Sycosis/ Syphilis)

Obstruction

- Abdominal cramps, bloating, distension, nausea, vomiting, borborygmy (Psora)
- Luminal narrowing secondary to inflammation- reversible (Psora)
- Luminal narrowing secondary to fibrosis / scarring – irreversible (Psora/ Sycosis)

Fistulization

- **Entero-enteric fistula-** asymptomatic (Psora/ Syphilis)
- **Entero-vesical fistula-** frequent urinary tract infections and dysuria, pneumaturia (Psora/ Syphilis)

- **Entero-vaginal fistula-** passing air or fecal matter per vagina (Psora/ Syphilis)
- **Entero-cutaneous fistula-** tends to form in the path of least resistance
- **Perianal lesions-**
  - External perianal opening with drainage (Psora/ Syphilis)
  - Painful perianal swelling or abscess if external opening blocked (Psora/ Syphilis)

Perforation

- Resembling appendicitis, diverticulitis (Psora/ Sycosis/ Syphilis)

Ulcerative colitis

There are three common manifestations of ulcerative colitis-

- **Abdominal Cramps:** Often accompanied by diarrhea and urgency.
- **Rectal Bleeding:** Fresh blood in stool, with associated urgency and tenesmus.
- **Other Symptoms:** Mild fever, tachycardia, dehydration, abdominal tenderness, and blood on rectal examination are also observed. (Psora/ Syphilis)

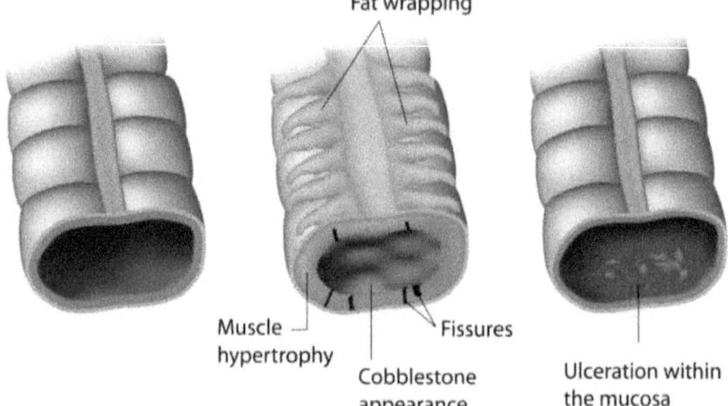

Fat wrapping
Muscle hypertrophy
Fissures
Cobblestone appearance
Ulceration within the mucosa

Diagnosis of Inflammatory Bowel Disease

Diagnosing inflammatory bowel disease (IBD) typically involves a combination of approaches, including:

Medical History

Gathering a thorough medical history from the patient, including symptoms, duration, and any relevant family history of gastrointestinal conditions.

Physical Examination

A physical examination to assess for signs of inflammation, such as abdominal tenderness or palpable masses.

Laboratory Tests

Blood tests to check for markers of inflammation, as well as to assess for anemia or nutritional deficiencies are needed. Stool tests may also be conducted to check for the presence of blood, infections, or inflammation.

Routine Laboratory Tests

- CRP C-reactive protein- non-specific inflammation
- ESR Erythrocyte Sedimentation Rate- non-specific inflammation
- CBC Complete Blood Count- Anemia, infection, inflammation
- Electrolytes Sodium, Potassium, Chloride, CO_2- Dehydration

- Liver Function Test- Liver Enzymes and medication side effects, PSC (primary sclerosing cholangitis)
- Vitamin B12- Anemia, nutritional status
- Vitamin D- Bone mineral status
- Calprotectin Stool protein- Active intestinal inflammation
- Lactoferrin Stool protein- Active intestinal inflammation
- pANCA perinuclear anti-neutrophil antibody- Distinguishes UC from CD
- ASCA anti-Saccharomyces cervisiae antibody- Distinguishes CD from UC
- CBir1 anti-flagellin antibody- Indicative of Crohn's disease
- OmpC anti-OmpC antibody- Indicative of Crohn's disease

Imaging Studies

Imaging tests such as endoscopy, colonoscopy, or imaging scans (e.g., CT scan, MRI) may be performed to visualize the gastrointestinal tract and identify any abnormalities, such as inflammation, ulcers, or strictures.

Biopsy

During endoscopy or colonoscopy, tissue samples (biopsies) may be taken from the gastrointestinal tract for examination under a microscope to confirm the presence of inflammation and distinguish between Crohn's disease and ulcerative colitis.

Tests for suspected IBD location or complication

- lleocolonic disease- Colonoscopy, SBFT/enteroclysis, CTE, MRE, capsule endoscopy (CE)
- Upper tract Crohn's disease- EGD-Upper GI Series (UGIS)
- Perianal Crohn's disease- MRI-EUS
- PSC (primary sclerosing cholangitis)- ERCP
- Pancreatic and bile ducts- MRCP
- Perforations, blockages, abscesses- Plain X-ray and CT scan

Overall, the diagnosis of IBD involves a comprehensive evaluation of clinical symptoms, laboratory findings, imaging studies, and histological examination to confirm the presence of inflammation and establish an accurate diagnosis. Treatment decisions are then based on the severity and extent of inflammation, as well as the specific subtype of IBD diagnosed.

Treatment of Inflammatory Bowel Disease

Inflammatory Bowel Disease (IBD), which includes Crohn's disease and ulcerative colitis, requires a comprehensive treatment plan tailored to the severity and location of the disease, as well as the individual patient's response to therapy. The main goals of IBD treatment are to reduce inflammation, achieve and maintain remission, and improve quality of life. Here are the primary treatment strategies:

Medications

Appropriate homoeopathic treatment is the best under guidance of an expert Homoeopath.

Nutritional Support

Dietary Adjustments: Specific diets like the low-residue diet, low-FODMAP diet, or specific carbohydrate diet can help manage symptoms.

Nutritional Supplements: May be necessary to address deficiencies (e.g., iron, vitamin B12, vitamin D, calcium).

Enteral Nutrition: Liquid diets are sometimes used, especially in pediatric patients, to induce remission.

Surgery

Indications: Surgery is indicated for complications like strictures, fistulas, abscesses, or when medical therapy fails.

Procedures for Crohn's Disease: Resection of diseased bowel segments, strictureplasty, or abscess drainage.

Procedures for Ulcerative Colitis: Total proctocolectomy with ileal pouch-anal anastomosis (IPAA) or ileostomy.

Lifestyle and Supportive Care

Smoking Cessation: Especially important for patients with Crohn's disease, as smoking worsens the disease.

Stress Management: Techniques like mindfulness, meditation, and therapy can help manage stress, which may exacerbate symptoms.

Regular Monitoring: Frequent check-ups to monitor disease activity, side effects of medications, and nutritional status.

Complementary and Alternative Therapies

Probiotics: May help in maintaining remission, especially in ulcerative colitis.

Omega-3 Fatty Acids: Some evidence suggests anti-inflammatory benefits.

Herbal Supplements: Used by some patients, though evidence for efficacy is limited and should be used with caution.

Vaccinations and Preventive Care

Vaccinations: Important to prevent infections, especially in immunosuppressed patients.

Cancer Screening: Regular screenings for colorectal cancer in patients with long-standing ulcerative colitis or Crohn's colitis.

Personalized Treatment Plans

Treatment plans for IBD are highly personalized and require ongoing adjustments based on disease activity, response to treatments, and the presence of complications. Multidisciplinary care involving gastroenterologists, surgeons, nutritionists, and mental health professionals is often necessary to provide comprehensive care.

Conclusion

The treatment of IBD involves a combination of medications, nutritional support, lifestyle modifications, and sometimes surgery. The primary goal is to reduce inflammation, achieve and maintain remission, and improve the patient's quality of life. Regular monitoring and a personalized approach to treatment are essential for effective management of this chronic condition.

Upon thorough examination of inflammatory bowel disease (IBD), it becomes evident that it transcends mere localized issues, delving into the realm of genetics and constitutional disharmony. The individual, in entirety, is impacted by the underlying factors contributing to IBD, as well as by the repercussions of the established disease, both physically and mentally. Therefore, addressing IBD necessitates a holistic approach that encompasses the entire person, rather than focusing solely on the gastrointestinal system.

Utilizing a well-selected constitutional remedy, adhering to the principles of similia, often yields a permanent resolution of the condition. This underscores the importance of treating the individual as a whole, aiming to restore balance and harmony to their overall health and well-being.

Part- Two

Irritable Bowel Syndrome

Historical Review of Irritable Bowel Syndrome

The journey of discovery and research evolution in Irritable Bowel Syndrome (IBS) extends across centuries, punctuated by pivotal milestones and groundbreaking discoveries. Here's a brief historical timeline of Irritable Bowel Syndrome (IBS):

Ancient Times

References to symptoms resembling IBS can be found in ancient medical texts from civilizations such as Mesopotamia, Egypt, Greece, and Rome. However, the understanding of the condition was rudimentary, often attributed to disturbances in bodily humors or diet-related issues.

19th Century

The concept of "nervous diarrhea" emerged during this period, suggesting a connection between gastrointestinal symptoms and nervous system function. Physicians began to recognize the role of psychological factors in gastrointestinal disorders.

Early 20th Century

The term "spastic colon" was coined to describe the symptoms of abdominal pain and altered bowel habits seen in IBS. However, medical understanding of the condition remained limited, and treatment options were largely symptomatic.

Mid to Late 20th Century

Medical research into IBS expanded, with advancements in diagnostic techniques and a growing understanding of gastrointestinal physiology. Studies began to explore the role of motility disorders, visceral hypersensitivity, and psychosocial factors in IBS pathogenesis.

21st Century

IBS gained recognition as a multifactorial disorder influenced by genetic, environmental, and psychosocial factors. The Rome criteria, a set of standardized diagnostic criteria, were established to aid in the diagnosis of IBS. Research into the gut microbiota, immune system dysregulation, and central nervous system interactions continues to deepen our understanding of IBS pathophysiology.

Throughout history, the perception and understanding of IBS have evolved significantly, leading to improved diagnosis, management, and quality of life for individuals affected by this complex disorder.

Definition of Irritable Bowel Syndrome

Irritable Bowel Syndrome (IBS) is a chronic gastrointestinal disorder characterized by a group of symptoms that commonly include abdominal pain, bloating, cramping, and changes in bowel habits, such as diarrhea, constipation, or alternating between the two. It's a functional disorder, meaning there's no visible evidence of disease in the digestive tract.

The exact cause of IBS is not fully understood, but it's believed to involve a combination of factors, including abnormal contractions of the colon and intestines, heightened sensitivity to pain in the digestive system, and disturbances in the gut-brain axis, which involves communication between the brain and the gut. Factors such as genetics, diet, stress, infections, and changes in gut bacteria composition may also play a role in triggering or exacerbating symptoms.

IBS is classified into different subtypes based on predominant symptoms, including IBS with diarrhea (IBS-D), IBS with constipation (IBS-C), mixed IBS (IBS-M), and unsubtyped IBS (IBS-U).

Diagnosing IBS involves ruling out other medical conditions that can cause similar symptoms through a thorough medical history, physical examination, and sometimes additional tests, such as blood tests, stool tests, and imaging studies. The Rome criteria, a set of symptom-based criteria, are commonly used to diagnose IBS.

Treatment for IBS is targeted on managing symptoms and improving quality of life. This may involve dietary changes, such as increasing fiber intake or following a low FODMAP diet, lifestyle modifications, stress management techniques, and medications to relieve specific symptoms, such as antispasmodics for abdominal pain or diarrhea, laxatives for constipation, or antidepressants for mood-related symptoms.

While IBS is a chronic condition that can significantly impact a person's life, it's not life-threatening and doesn't lead to serious complications, such as intestinal bleeding or cancer. With proper management and lifestyle adjustments, many people with IBS can effectively control their symptoms and lead fulfilling lives.

Pathophysiology of Irritable Bowel Syndrome

The pathophysiology of Irritable Bowel Syndrome (IBS) is complex and not entirely understood, involving various factors that contribute to the development and perpetuation of symptoms. Several mechanisms have been proposed, although none fully explain the entire spectrum of IBS manifestations.

Altered Gut Motility

One prominent theory suggests that abnormalities in gut motility play a significant role in IBS. This includes both hypermotility (increased intestinal contractions leading to diarrhea) and hypomotility (reduced intestinal contractions causing constipation). Dysregulated contractions can result in changes in bowel habits, a hallmark feature of IBS.

Visceral Hypersensitivity

Individuals with IBS often exhibit heightened sensitivity to visceral stimuli, such as distension or contraction of the intestines. This visceral hypersensitivity can lead to increased perception of pain and discomfort in response to normal intestinal function, contributing to abdominal pain and discomfort characteristic of IBS.

Gut-Brain Axis Dysfunction

The gut-brain axis, which involves bidirectional communication between the central nervous system (CNS) and the gastrointestinal tract, plays a crucial role in regulating gut function and visceral sensitivity. Dysregulation of this axis, possibly due to stress, psychological factors, or alterations in neurotransmitter signaling, may contribute to the pathophysiology of IBS.

Intestinal Inflammation and Immune Activation

Low-grade inflammation and immune activation in the gut have been implicated in some cases of IBS, particularly in subsets of patients with post-infectious IBS (PI-IBS). Infections or other insults to the gastrointestinal mucosa can trigger an abnormal immune response, leading to persistent inflammation and symptom development in susceptible individuals.

Gut Microbiota Dysbiosis

Alterations in the composition and function of the gut microbiota, known as dysbiosis, have been observed in some individuals with IBS. Changes in microbial diversity, abundance of specific bacterial species, and metabolic activity may influence gut motility, immune function, and visceral sensitivity, contributing to IBS symptoms.

Serotonin Metabolism and IBS

Most of the body's serotonin is stored in intestinal enterochromaffin cells. These cells act as sensory transducers for intra-luminal stimuli and release serotonin, which activates neurons, regulates gastrointestinal motility, and influences CNS signaling. The enterochromaffin cells are increased in individuals with post-infectious IBS compared to those who recovered from acute enteric infections.

Psychological Factors

Psychological factors, such as stress, anxiety, and depression, can exacerbate IBS symptoms and contribute to disease onset and progression. The bidirectional interaction between the brain and the gut, known as the gut-brain axis, can modulate gut function and sensitivity in response to emotional stimuli. Overall, the pathophysiology of IBS is multifactorial and likely involves interactions between genetic, environmental, microbial, immune, and psychosocial factors.

Gut gas and IBS

Excessive gut gas, also known as flatulence, is a common symptom associated with Irritable Bowel Syndrome (IBS). In individuals with IBS, disturbances in gut motility, visceral hypersensitivity, and alterations in the gut microbiota can contribute to the production and accumulation of gas in the intestines. It may also alter the gut mobility in turn.

Dietary Factors

Dietary components that are poorly absorbed in the small intestine, such as certain carbohydrates (e.g., fermentable oligosaccharides, disaccharides, monosaccharides, and polyols, known as FODMAPs), can undergo fermentation by gut bacteria in the colon, leading to gas production. Foods high in FODMAPs, such as certain fruits, vegetables, grains, and dairy products, may exacerbate symptoms of bloating and gas in individuals with IBS.

Swallowed Air

In addition to gas produced within the intestines, swallowing air (aerophagia) can also contribute to gut gas accumulation. Individuals with IBS may swallow more air than usual, particularly during episodes of anxiety or stress, which can further exacerbate symptoms of bloating and discomfort.

Genetic Evidence for IBS

Research indicates that Irritable Bowel Syndrome (IBS) may have a genetic component. Studies have observed that IBS tends to run in families, and twin studies have demonstrated a higher concordance rate in monozygotic twins compared to dizygotic twins, suggesting a genetic influence. Additionally, a mutation in the SCN5A gene, which encodes the voltage-gated sodium channel type V (alpha subunit) linked to congenital prolonged QT syndrome, has been associated with abdominal pain. This particular sodium channel is present in the interstitial cells of Cajal and the circular smooth muscle of the human gastrointestinal tract.

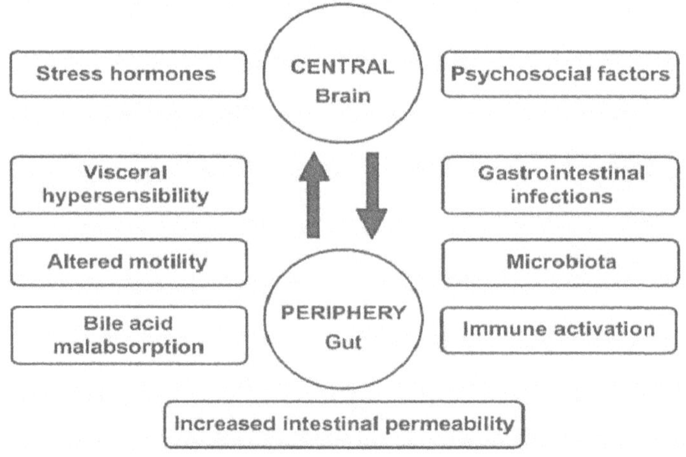

Etiology of Irritable Bowel Syndrome

The exact cause of Irritable Bowel Syndrome (IBS) is not fully understood, but it is believed to result from a combination of several factors. Key potential causes include:

Genetic Factors

Genetics may play a role in IBS, as it often runs in families. Specific gene mutations, such as those affecting the serotonin transporter or voltage-gated sodium channels, have been associated with IBS.

Gut-Brain Axis Dysregulation

The communication between the brain and the gastrointestinal tract, known as the gut-brain axis, can be disrupted in IBS. This dysregulation affects gut motility, secretion, and sensitivity, leading to symptoms.

Visceral Hypersensitivity

Many IBS patients have an increased sensitivity to intestinal pain and discomfort. This heightened sensitivity, known as visceral hypersensitivity, causes normal digestive processes to be perceived as painful.

Abnormal Gastrointestinal Motility

IBS is often associated with irregular muscle contractions in the intestines. These abnormalities can cause rapid transit (resulting in diarrhea), slow transit (leading to constipation), or a combination of both.

Microbiome Imbalance

An imbalance in the gut microbiota, known as dysbiosis, is common in IBS. This imbalance can influence digestion, immune function, and the production of gas and other substances that affect gut health.

Post-Infectious Changes

IBS can develop after a severe gastrointestinal infection, known as post-infectious IBS. This may be due to changes in the gut microbiota, immune activation, and ongoing low-grade inflammation following the infection.

Serotonin Dysregulation

Serotonin (5-HT) is crucial for regulating gut motility and sensation. Abnormalities in serotonin levels and its receptor function can contribute to the symptoms of IBS.

Immune System Activation

Some individuals with IBS exhibit low-grade inflammation and immune activation in the gut. This can be triggered by infections, food sensitivities, or other factors, leading to the release of inflammatory mediators that affect gut function.

Psychological Factors

Stress, anxiety, and depression are common in IBS sufferers and can exacerbate symptoms. The relationship between psychological factors and IBS is bidirectional, with stress and mental health influencing gut function and vice versa.

Dietary Triggers

Certain foods can trigger IBS symptoms. Common dietary triggers include high-fat foods, caffeine, alcohol, and FODMAPs (fermentable oligosaccharides, disaccharides, monosaccharides, and polyols).

Hormonal Changes

Hormonal fluctuations, particularly in women, can influence IBS symptoms. Many women report that their symptoms worsen during menstrual periods.

Understanding these potential causes helps in identifying and managing triggers for IBS, thereby improving treatment outcomes and quality of life for those affected by the condition.

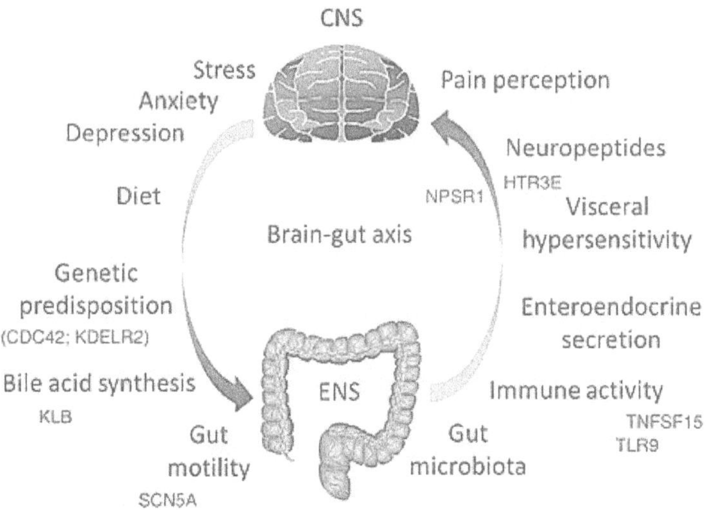

Types of Irritable Bowel Syndrome

Irritable Bowel Syndrome (IBS) is classified into several types based on the predominant bowel habit symptoms. These types help in guiding specific treatments and management strategies. The main types of IBS are:

IBS with Predominant Constipation (IBS-C)

Symptoms: Hard or lumpy stools at least 25% of the time and loose or watery stools less than 25% of the time.

Characteristics: Patients often experience infrequent bowel movements, straining during defecation, and a sense of incomplete evacuation.

IBS with Predominant Diarrhea (IBS-D)

Symptoms: Loose or watery stools at least 25% of the time and hard or lumpy stools less than 25% of the time.

Characteristics: Patients typically have frequent, urgent bowel movements, abdominal pain, and discomfort that are often relieved by defecation.

IBS with Mixed Bowel Habits (IBS-M)

Symptoms: Both hard or lumpy stools and loose or watery stools are present at least 25% of the time.

Characteristics: Patients experience alternating periods of constipation and diarrhea, along with abdominal pain and bloating.

IBS Unclassified (IBS-U)

Symptoms: Patients who do not fit into the above categories, having irregular stool patterns that do not consistently meet the criteria for IBS-C, IBS-D, or IBS-M.

Characteristics: Symptoms can vary widely, and patients may not exhibit a clear pattern of constipation or diarrhea.

Each type of IBS requires a tailored approach to management and treatment, considering the predominant symptoms and their impact on the patient's quality of life. Medications, dietary modifications, and lifestyle changes are often recommended based on the specific IBS subtype.

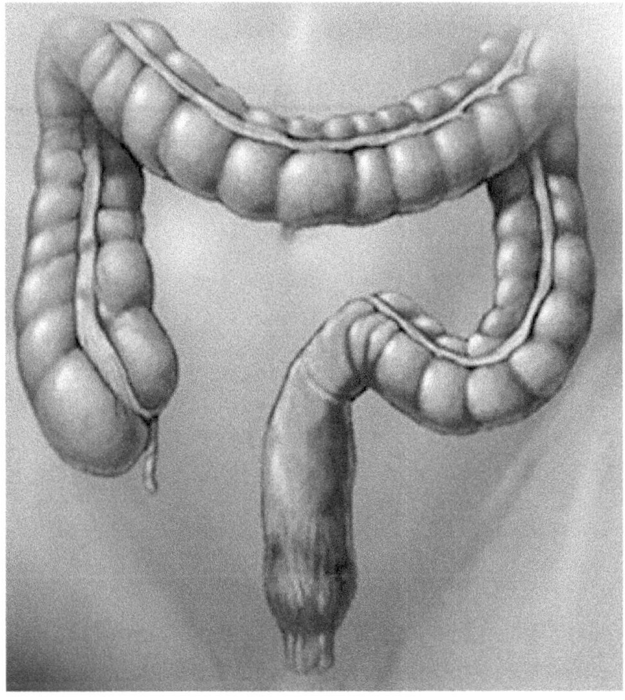

Signs and symptoms of Irritable Bowel Syndrome

Irritable Bowel Syndrome (IBS) is characterized by a variety of gastrointestinal symptoms that can vary in intensity and frequency among individuals. The most common signs and symptoms include:

Abdominal Pain and Cramping

Location: Typically experienced in the lower abdomen but can occur anywhere in the abdomen.

Nature: Often described as cramping, sharp, or aching.

Modality: Pain usually lessens after a bowel movement.

Bloating and flatulence

Bloating: A feeling of fullness or swelling in the abdomen.

Gas: Increased passing of gas (flatulence) is common.

Altered Bowel Habits

Diarrhea (IBS-D): Frequent, loose, or watery stools.

Constipation (IBS-C): Infrequent, hard, or lumpy stools.

Mixed (IBS-M): Alternating between diarrhea and constipation.

Unclassified (IBS-U): Symptoms that do not fit neatly into the above categories.

Changes in Stool Appearance

Consistency: Stools may vary from hard and pellet-like to loose and watery.

Color: Normal stool color is typically brown, but dietary changes and medications can affect color.

Mucus in Stool

Observation: Some people with IBS notice mucus in their stool, which can be clear or white.

Urgency and Incomplete Evacuation

Urgency: A sudden, strong urge to have a bowel movement.

Incomplete Evacuation: Feeling that the bowel movement was incomplete, even after going to the bathroom.

Other Gastrointestinal Symptoms

Nausea: Some individuals experience nausea, especially after meals.

Heartburn: A burning sensation in the chest or upper abdomen.

Non-Gastrointestinal Symptoms

Fatigue: A general feeling of tiredness or low energy.

Sleep Disturbances: Trouble falling asleep or staying asleep.

Headaches: Recurring headaches or migraines.

Triggers and Exacerbating Factors

Some factors can activate or worsen IBS symptoms, including:

Dietary Triggers: Foods high in FODMAPs, fatty foods, caffeine, alcohol, and spicy foods.

Stress and Anxiety: Psychological stress can exacerbate IBS symptoms.

Hormonal Changes: Women may experience worse symptoms during menstruation.

Medications: Certain medications can trigger or worsen symptoms.

Impact on Quality of Life

IBS can significantly affect a person's quality of life, leading to:

Social and Emotional Stress

Worrying about symptom flare-ups can lead to anxiety and depression.

Work and Daily Activities

Frequent symptoms can interfere with work, school, and daily activities.

Recognizing these signs and symptoms is crucial for the diagnosis and management of IBS, helping individuals seek appropriate treatment and lifestyle modifications to manage their condition effectively.

Diagnosis of Irritable Bowel Syndrome

Diagnosing Irritable Bowel Syndrome (IBS) involves a combination of evaluating symptoms, ruling out other conditions, and sometimes using specific diagnostic criteria. The process typically includes the following steps:

Medical History and Symptom Review

Detailed History: The doctor will take a comprehensive medical history, focusing on the nature, duration, and frequency of symptoms such as abdominal pain, bloating, and changes in bowel habits.

Symptom Patterns: Identifying whether symptoms are related to bowel movements, diet, or stress can provide important clues.

Physical Examination

Abdominal Exam: A physical examination of the abdomen to check for tenderness, bloating, or other abnormalities.

Rectal Exam: In some cases, a digital rectal examination may be performed to check for lumps or other rectal problems.

Diagnostic Criteria

Rome IV Criteria: IBS is often diagnosed using the Rome IV criteria, which include:

- Recurrent abdominal pain, on average, at least one day per week in the last three months.

- Associated with two or more of the following:
    - Related to defecation.
    - Associated with a change in the frequency of stool.
    - Associated with a change in the form (appearance) of stool.

Exclusion of Other Conditions

Blood Tests: To check for anemia, infection, and inflammation markers, such as a complete blood count (CBC) and C-reactive protein (CRP) levels.

Stool Tests: To check for infections, parasites, and blood in the stool.

Lactose Intolerance Tests: To determine if symptoms are related to lactose intolerance.

Celiac Disease Screening: Blood tests to rule out celiac disease, which can cause similar symptoms.

Additional Diagnostic Procedures

Colonoscopy or Sigmoidoscopy: Recommended if there are alarm features such as unexplained weight loss, gastrointestinal bleeding, or significant changes in bowel habits, especially in individuals over 50 or with a family history of colorectal cancer.

Imaging Studies: Abdominal X-rays, CT scans, or ultrasounds may be used to rule out other abdominal issues.

Breath Tests

Hydrogen Breath Test: To identify bacterial overgrowth or carbohydrate malabsorption, such as lactose or fructose intolerance.

Red Flags and Alarm Features of IBS

Certain symptoms may suggest conditions other than IBS and warrant further investigation:

- Unintentional weight loss.
- Rectal bleeding or blood in the stool.
- Anemia or other signs of systemic illness.
- Persistent pain not relieved by bowel movements.
- Family history of colorectal cancer, inflammatory bowel disease, or celiac disease.

Conclusion

The diagnosis of IBS is primarily clinical, based on symptom patterns and the exclusion of other conditions. Using established criteria such as the Rome IV guidelines helps ensure an accurate diagnosis, allowing for appropriate management and treatment strategies. Regular follow-up and reassessment may be necessary to address ongoing symptoms and adjust treatment plans.

Treatment of Irritable Bowel Syndrome

Treatment for Irritable Bowel Syndrome (IBS) is individualized, focusing on relieving symptoms and improving quality of life. The approach often involves a combination of dietary modifications, lifestyle changes, pharmacotherapy, and psychological therapies. Here are the main treatment strategies:

Dietary Modifications

Low FODMAP Diet: Reducing intake of fermentable oligosaccharides, disaccharides, monosaccharides, and polyols (FODMAPs) can alleviate symptoms for many patients.

Fiber Intake

IBS-C: Increasing soluble fiber (e.g., psyllium) can help improve constipation.

IBS-D: Reducing insoluble fiber may decrease diarrhea.

Hydration: Adequate water intake is important, especially for those with constipation.

Avoiding Trigger Foods: Identifying and avoiding foods that trigger symptoms, such as caffeine, alcohol, fatty foods, and gas-producing foods like beans and carbonated drinks.

Lifestyle Changes

Regular Exercise: Physical activity can improve bowel function and reduce stress.

Stress Management: Techniques such as yoga, meditation, and deep breathing exercises can help manage stress, which can exacerbate IBS symptoms.

Sleep Hygiene: Ensuring adequate and quality sleep can help manage symptoms.

Pharmacotherapy

Antispasmodics: Remedies like Mag phos, Belladonna, Colocynthcan etc. help reduce abdominal pain and cramping.

Laxatives: For IBS-C, osmotic laxatives (e.g., polyethylene glycol) can relieve constipation.

Antidiarrheals: For IBS-D, remedies like Podophyllum, Croton tig, Gambogia, Arg nit, Gels, Mag carb, Nat carb, Oleander etc.

Antidepressants: Passiflora, Ignatia, Sepia, Nat mur, Gels, Bufo, Ars alb, Puls etc. can help with pain and coexisting depression or anxiety.

Probiotics: Certain strains of probiotics may help balance gut microbiota and reduce symptoms.

Prescription Medications

Homoeopathic medicine as per symptoms.

Psychological Therapies

Cognitive Behavioral Therapy (CBT): Can help manage stress and alter negative thought patterns that exacerbate symptoms.

Gut-Directed Hypnotherapy: Focuses on relaxing the gut through guided imagery and relaxation techniques.

Counseling and Support Groups: Talking with a therapist or joining a support group can provide emotional support and coping strategies.

Complementary and Alternative Therapies

Acupuncture: Some patients find symptom relief through acupuncture.

Herbal Remedies: Certain herbs like peppermint oil can help reduce pain and bloating.

Personalized Treatment Approach

IBS treatment is highly individualized. Patients may need to try several different treatments to find what works best for them. Regular follow-up with a holistic physician is essential to monitor symptoms and adjust treatment plans as needed.

Conclusion

Effective management of IBS typically requires a multifaceted approach. Combining dietary modifications, lifestyle changes, Homoepathic therapy, and psychological support can significantly improve symptoms and quality of life for many patients. Collaboration between patients and healthcare providers is key to developing an effective, personalized treatment plan.

Common Homoeopathic remedies for IBD and IBS

abrom-a. Abrot. Acal. Acet-ac. achy-a. Acon-c. ACON. Act-sp. adren. aesc. Aeth. aethi-a. agar-ph. AGAR. Agn. agra. ail. alet. alf. All-c. all-s. allox. aln. ALOE alst. alum-p. alum-sil. ALUM. Alumn. Am-c. AM-M. am-p. Ambr. ammc. anac-oc. Anac. anag. anan. androg-p. ang. Ango. anh. Anis. ANT-C. Ant-t. anth. aphis APIS Apoc-a. APOC. aral. Aran. arb. arg-cy. ARG-MET. Arg-n. Arg-o. arge. arist-cl. ARN. Ars-i. ars-s-f. ars-s-r. ARS. arthr-u. Arum-t. arund. ASAF. Asar. asc-c. asc-t. asim. astac. aster. atis. atro. aur-ar. aur-fu. aur-i. Aur-m-n. aur-m. aur-s. AUR. bac. BAPT. BAR-C. bar-i. Bar-m. bar-s. baros. bell-p. BELL. BENZ-AC. berb-a. Berb. bism. Bol-la. bold. BORX. BOV. Brom. BRY. bufo but-ac. cact. cadm-met. cadm-s. cain. caj. cal-ren. Calad. calc-act. calc-ar. calc-chln. Calc-f. Calc-hp. calc-i. CALC-P. calc-s. calc-sil. CALC. Camph. cann-i. cann-s. Cann-xyz. Canth. CAPS. Carb-ac. Carb-an. CARB-V. carbn-dox. carbn-o. CARBN-S. carc. card-b. Card-m. Carl. Casc. cassia-s. castm. castor-eq. catar. Caul. CAUST. cean. Cedr. cench. cere-b. CHAM. chap. CHEL. chen-v. Chin-b. CHIN. CHININ-AR. Chinin-s. chion. Chlf. chlol. chlor. Chloram. chol. Cic. cimic. Cimx. cina cinch. cinnb. cist. Cit-v. Clem. cob-n. Cob. coc-c. Coca COCC. Coch. Coff. COLCH. COLL. COLOC. colocin. com. Con. conv. convo-s. Cop. Cor-r. Corn. cortiso. cot. coxs. croc. Crot-c. Crot-h. CROT-T. cub. Cupr-act. Cupr-ar. CUPR. Cycl. cyn-d. cyt-l. daph. der. Dig. DIOS. Diosm. dirc. dol. Dros. DULC. eberth. Echi. echit. elaps ELAT. epig. epil. equis-h. erech. erig. ery-a. eryt-j. eucal. euon-

a. euon. euonin. **Eup-a.** eup-per. eup-pur. **EUPH. Euphr.** eupi. eys. fab. fago. fel **FERR-AR.** ferr-cy. **Ferr-i.** ferr-p. ferr-s. **Ferr.** ferul. fil. fl-ac. flor-p. form. frag. fuch. fuma-ac. gaert. gal-ac. gali. **GAMB.** gast. **GELS.** gent-c. geo. **Gins.** glon. glyc. **Glycyr-g.** gnaph. **Gran. GRAPH. GRAT. Guaj.** guat. haem. ham. hed. hedeo. **HELL. Helon. Hep.** hip-ac. hipp. **Hippoz.** hir. hist. hoit. hom-xyz. hura **HYDR.** hydrang. hydrc. **Hydrin-m. HYOS. Hyper.** Ichth. **IGN.** ind. **Iod.** iodof. **IP.** ipom-p. **IRIS** Iris-t. jab. jac-c. **Jal. JATR-C. Jug-c.** jug-r. **KALI-AR. KALI-BI. Kali-br. Kali-c. KALI-CHL. Kali-i. Kali-m. Kali-n.** kali-p. **Kali-pic. KALI-S.** kali-sil. **KALM. Kreos.** kurch. **Lac-ac. Lac-c. Lac-d.** lacer. **LACH.** lact. lappa lat-m. **LAUR. Lec. Led. Lept.** liat. lil-t. **Lim.** lipp. **LITH-C.** lob. luf-op. **LYC.** lycps-v. lyss. m-ambo. **M-arct.** m-aust. **Mag-c. MAG-M. MAG-P. Mag-s. Manc.** mand. mang-act. mang-s. **Mang. Med.** mentho. **Meny.** meph. **MERC-C. Merc-cy. Merc-d.** merc-i-f. merc-i-r. merc-sul. **MERC.** merl. **Mez.** micr. mill. mim-p. morph. **Mosch. MUR-AC.** murx. myric. nabal. naja narc-ps. **Nat-ar.** nat-br. **NAT-C.** nat-f. nat-hchls. **NAT-M.** nat-n. **Nat-p. NAT-S.** nat-sal. nicc. **NIT-AC.** nit-m-ac. nit-s-d. **Nuph. NUX-M. NUX-V.** oci-sa. oci. ol-an. ol-j. **OLND.** onis. onos. **OP.** opun-s. oreo. osm. ox-ac. oxyd. oxyg. oxyt. oxyte-chl. p-benzq. paeon. pall. **Par.** paraf. **PAREIR.** penic. **Petr. PH-AC.** phel. phlor. **PHOS. Phyt.** pic-ac. pin-s. pipe. **Plan. Plat. Plb-act.** plb-chr. plb-xyz. **PLB. PODO.** polyg-h. pot-e. **Prun.** psil. **PSOR. Ptel. PULS. PYROG.** quas. rad-br. **Ran-b.** ran-s. **Raph.** rat. rauw. rham-cal. rham-cath. **Rheum Rhod. Rhus-g. RHUS-T.** rhus-v. ric. rob. rub-t. **Rumx. Ruta** sabad. sabal sabin. sacch. sal-ac. samb. **Sang.** sanic. saroth. **SARS.** scroph-xyz. sec. **Sel. Semp.** senec. **Seneg. SENN. SEP.**

SIL. sin-n. sol-ni. sol-t-ae. solid. sphing. SPIG. spira. SPONG. Squil. Stann. Staph. stel. stict. Stigm. Stram. Streptoc. STRONT-C. STRY. SUL-AC. sul-i. sulfa. sulfonam. SULPH. sumb. syph. Tab. TARAX. Tarent. tell. TER. teucr. thal-met. thal-s. ther. thlas. THUJ. thymol. thyr. til. toxo-g. Trios. Trom. tub-r. Tub. uran-met. Uran-n. urt-u. uva VALER. vanad. vario. Verat-v. VERAT. verb. vesi. vesp. vib. vichy-g. vinc. viol-t. vip. visc. x-ray yohim. zinc-fcy. zinc-p. Zinc-s. zinc-val. Zinc. ZING.

Short repertory of IBD and IBS

ABDOMEN - DISTENSION – painful ACON. Aeth. alum. ant-t. arg-met. ARS. Bar-c. bell. Bry. calad. canth. CAUST. cham. chin. cic. croc. Euph. hedeo. hell. Hyos. ign. ip. kali-bi. kali-c. kali-i. kali-p. LACH. mag-p. merc-c. MERC. mez. nat-c. nat-m. nit-ac. nux-v. petr. raph. rhod. RHUS-T. sabin. sep. sphing. spig. stann. stram. stront-c. sulph. valer. verat.

ABDOMEN - FATTY DEGENERATION of liver aur. calc-f. chel. kali-bi. kali-s. lac-d. Lyc. lyss. mang-act. mang. Merc. phlor. Phos. pic-ac. vanad.

ABDOMEN – GALLSTONES ARS. aur. bapt. bell. berb. bold. Bry. calc-f. calc. card-m. Cham. chel. chin. chion. chlf. chol. coloc. cupr. dig. dios. eberth. euon-a. euon. euonin. fab. fel ferr-s. fuma-ac. gels. guat. hed. Hydr. jug-c. lach. Lept. lith-c. lob. lyc. mag-p. mag-s. mand. mang. merc-d. MERC. myric. nat-s. nat-sal. nit-s-d. nux-v. Phos. podo. ptel. sang. sulph. tarax. thlas. verat. vichy-g.

ABDOMEN - INFLAMMATION – Cecum acon. APIS arn. Ars. bapt. BELL. BRY. Calad. canth. Card-m. Chin. Colch. coll. Coloc. Crot-h. Dios. Echi. ferr-p. gamb. gast. gins. hep. iris-t. kali-m. LACH. Lyc. Merc-c. MERC. Nat-s. Nux-v. OP. Phos. plb-xyz. Plb. pyrog. rham-cal. rham-cath. RHUS-T. Samb. Sep. Sil. Stram. sulph. THUJ. verat.

ABDOMEN - INFLAMMATION - Colon - accompanied by – flatulence arg-n.

ABDOMEN - INFLAMMATION - Colon - accompanied by – hemorrhage aran. cyn-d. ham. merc-c. merc. streptoc.

ABDOMEN - INFLAMMATION - Colon - accompanied by - sexual desire; increased gamb. Grat. lyc. nabal.

ABDOMEN - INFLAMMATION - Colon - accompanied by – weakness cadm-s.

ABDOMEN - INFLAMMATION - Colon – acute achy-a. podo.

ABDOMEN - INFLAMMATION - Colon – amoebic ars. atis. kali-bi. kali-c. kurch. lach. merc-c. merc. nat-s. nux-v. sulph. thuj.

ABDOMEN - INFLAMMATION - Colon – cancerous mag-c. mag-m. mag-s. phos.

ABDOMEN - INFLAMMATION - Colon - chilliness; with cadm-s.

ABDOMEN - INFLAMMATION - Colon – chronic gaert. lyc. oxyte-chl. podo. sulph.

ABDOMEN - INFLAMMATION - Colon - diarrhea - amel. lach.

ABDOMEN - INFLAMMATION - Colon - flora; with pathological intestinal all-s.

ABDOMEN - INFLAMMATION - Colon - grief; after Ign. mag-c. mag-m. mag-s. nat-m. nat-s. Staph.

ABDOMEN - INFLAMMATION - Colon – membranous colch.

ABDOMEN - INFLAMMATION - Colon – mucous aethi-a. asar. aur-m-n. cop. coxs. graph. hell. hydr. merc-c. merc. pot-e. x-ray

ABDOMEN - INFLAMMATION - Colon – painful coloc. merc-c. merc. rhus-t.

ABDOMEN - INFLAMMATION - Colon - radiotherapy; after podo.

ABDOMEN - INFLAMMATION - Colon - summer agg. ip. kali-bi. puls.

ABDOMEN - INFLAMMATION - Colon – ulcerative Chloram. coloc. Hell. lil-t. Mag-s. merc. Nat-s. nit-ac. nux-v. podo. Streptoc. sulph. ter. zinc.

ABDOMEN - INFLAMMATION – Colon all-s. arg-n. ars. asaf. asar. bism. cadm-s. calc-ar. canth. caps. carc. cench. chin. colch. cop. crot-t. Ferr-i. Gamb. guat. hell. hoit. kali-bi. kali-n. kali-p. lach. lil-t. lyc. mag-c. MERC-C. merc. nat-c. nat-m. nat-s. nit-ac. nux-v. olnd. petr. ph-ac. phos. podo. ptel. raph. rhus-t. sulph. syph. ter. tub. verat. zinc-val. zinc.

ABDOMEN - INFLAMMATION - Liver – chronic Arn. aur. bell. carc. Card-m. Corn. crot-h. Lach. lact. LYC. mag-m. nat-c. Nat-m. NAT-S. Nit-ac. Nux-v. Phos. phyt. podo. Psor. ptel. ran-s. sel. sil. Sulph.

ABDOMEN - INFLAMMATION – Liver ACON. act-sp. aloe alum. am-c. ambr. anan. androg-p. ant-c. apis arg-n. Arn. ars-i. ARS. astac. aur-m. Aur. bapt. BELL. Brom. Bry. calc-f. Calc. Camph. cann-xyz. canth. Caps. carc. Card-m. Cham. CHEL. Chin. cic. cocc. Corn. crot-h. cupr. dig. Diosm. dol. eup-per. flor-p. graph. guat. Hep. Hippoz. ign. iod. kali-ar. kali-bi. Kali-c. kali-chl. kali-i. kali-n. kali-p. Lach. Laur. LYC. mag-c. Mag-m. mand. mang-s. mang. merc-d. Merc. nat-ar. nat-c. Nat-m. NAT-S. Nit-ac. nit-m-ac. nux-m. NUX-V. p-benzq. petr. ph-ac. Phos. phyt.

Podo. Psor. Ptel. puls. ran-b. ran-s. sang. scroph-xyz. sec. sel. sep. Sil. stann. staph. stel. sulfa. Sulph. tab.

ABDOMEN – INFLAMMATION Acet-ac. ACON. aloe alumn. ant-c. ANT-T. APIS arg-n. Arn. ars-i. ARS. asc-c. atro. Bapt. BELL. brom. BRY. bufo Cact. calc-sil. Calc. Canth. Carb-v. card-m. Cham. chin. cic. cocc. coff. COLCH. Coloc. Crot-c. Crot-h. cupr. Echi. euph. ferr-ar. ferr-p. Ferr. gamb. Gels. graph. guaj. HYOS. iod. Ip. kali-ar. kali-bi. Kali-c. Kali-chl. kali-i. Kali-n. kali-p. LACH. LAUR. LYC. med. Merc-c. Merc. Mez. Nux-v. Op. Ox-ac. PHOS. plb. podo. Puls. PYROG. RHUS-T. sabin. Sec. Sil. spong. squil. Stram. Sulph. TER. thuj. tub. uran-met. Uran-n. urt-u. Verat-v. Verat. vip.

ABDOMEN - PAIN – cramping Abrot. acal. acet-ac. Acon. adren. aesc. aeth. AGAR. ail. alet. all-c. ALOE alum-p. alum-sil. Alum. Alumn. Am-c. AM-M. ambr. ammc. Anac. anan. ang. Ango. anis. Ant-c. Ant-t. anth. aphis Apis apoc. aran. arg-cy. arg-met. Arg-n. arge. arist-cl. arn. ars-i. ars-s-f. ars-s-r. Ars. Asaf. Asar. aur-ar. aur-i. aur-m. aur-s. Aur. bapt. bar-c. bar-i. Bar-m. bar-s. BELL. Berb. Bism. Borx. Bov. brom. Bry. bufo but-ac. cact. Caj. calad. calc-i. Calc-p. calc-s. calc-sil. CALC. camph. cann-s. canth. caps. Carb-ac. Carb-an. CARB-V. carbn-dox. CARBN-S. card-b. card-m. carl. cassia-s. castm. catar. caul. Caust. cedr. cere-b. CHAM. CHEL. chen-v. Chin. chinin-ar. Cic. Cina cinch. cinnb. clem. cob. coc-c. COCC. Coff. Colch. coll. COLOC. colocin. Con. conv. Cop. corn. croc. crot-h. Crot-t. cub. Cupr-act. Cupr-ar. CUPR. Cycl. cyt-l. Dig. DIOS. dros. DULC. echi. echit. elaps Elat. erech. erig. eryt-j. Eup-per. eup-pur. Euph. Euphr. eupi. ferr-ar. ferr-p. Ferr. fil. gamb. Gels.

gent-c. glon. gnaph. Gran. GRAPH. Grat. guaj. guat. Ham. Hell. Hep. hist. Hydr. hydrc. Hyos. hyper. IGN. iod. IP. Iris Iris-t. jab. Jal. jatr-c. jug-r. kali-ar. Kali-bi. Kali-br. Kali-c. kali-i. kali-m. kali-n. kali-p. Kali-pic. Kali-s. kali-sil. Kreos. Lac-c. Lach. lact. lat-m. Laur. lec. Led. lept. liat. Lil-t. Lim. lob. luf-op. LYC. lycps-v. lyss. M-arct. m-aust. Mag-c. MAG-M. MAG-P. mag-s. manc. mand. mang. mentho. meny. merc-c. Merc. merl. Mez. micr. Morph. Mosch. Mur-ac. naja Nat-ar. Nat-c. nat-f. Nat-m. nat-p. Nat-s. nicc. Nit-ac. Nux-m. NUX-V. oci-sa. ol-j. olnd. onis. onos. OP. oreo. ox-ac. paeon. pall. Par. paraf. Petr. PH-AC. phel. phos. Phyt. Pic-ac. plan. Plat. Plb-act. plb-chr. PLB. PODO. polyg-h. prun. psor. ptel. PULS. pyrog. rad-br. Ran-b. ran-s. Raph. rat. rauw. Rheum rhod. Rhus-t. rhus-v. rob. Rumx. ruta sabad. sabin. samb. sang. saroth. sars. Sec. senec. seneg. SENN. Sep. SIL. Sin-n. Spig. spira. SPONG. squil. STANN. Staph. Stram. Stront-c. STRY. Sul-ac. sulfa. SULPH. sumb. tab. tarax. Tarent. tell. Ter. teucr. Thuj. trom. tub. Valer. verat-v. VERAT. verb. vesp. vib. viol-t. vip. zinc-fcy. zinc-p. Zinc. ZING.

ABDOMEN - PAIN - diarrhea – during Aeth. Agar. aloe alum. am-c. am-m. Anac. ang. ant-t. apoc. aran. Arg-n. arn. ars-i. Ars. asaf. asar. bapt. bar-c. Bell. bism. borx. bov. Bry. cact. calad. calc-p. calc. canth. caps. carb-an. carb-v. carbn-s. caust. cench. CHAM. Chin. chinin-ar. cimic. cob-n. cob. Cocc. Colch. COLOC. com. con. Cop. croc. Crot-t. cupr-ar. cupr. cycl. dig. DIOS. dros. dulc. euph. ferr-p. fl-ac. flor-p. fuch. GAMB. gels. Gran. graph. ham. hell. hep. hura ign. iod. Ip. iris jug-r. kali-ar. kali-bi. Kali-c. kali-i. kali-m. kali-n. kali-p. kali-s. lach. laur. Lyc. lycps-v. m-arct. m-aust. Mag-c. mag-m. mang.

Med. meny. MERC-C. merc-i-r. Merc. mez. mur-ac. nat-c. nat-m. Nat-s. nit-ac. Nux-v. op. ox-ac. petr. phos. plb. PODO. puls. Rheum rhus-t. rhus-v. rumx. sabad. sanic. sars. sec. senec. seneg. sep. sil. spig. spong. stann. staph. stram. stront-c. Sulph. tab. ter. THUJ. Trom. Verat. viol-t. zinc-s. zinc. zing.

ABDOMEN - PAIN - drawing pain abrot. acet-ac. acon. agar. agn. aloe alum. alumn. am-c. am-m. Anac. ang. ant-t. apis arg-n. ars-i. ars. asaf. aur-i. aur-m. aur. bar-c. bar-i. Bell. berb. borx. bov. bry. Calad. calc-s. Calc. camph. cann-s. CAPS. Carb-v. carbn-s. Card-m. caust. cham. chel. chin. cic. clem. cocc. colch. Coloc. con. croc. cupr-act. Cupr. dig. dros. ferr. gels. Gran. graph. grat. hell. Hep. hir. hyos. Ign. iod. jug-r. kali-ar. kali-c. kali-n. kreos. lach. Laur. led. Lyc. lyss. m-ambo. m-arct. m-aust. mag-c. Mag-m. mag-s. mang. meny. merc-c. merc. mez. mosch. murx. nat-ar. Nat-c. nat-m. nat-s. Nit-ac. Nux-v. op. par. petr. phos. Plat. plb. Podo. ptel. PULS. ran-b. rheum rhod. rhus-t. ruta sabin. sang. sars. sec. seneg. SEP. spig. spong. squil. stann. staph. stram. stront-c. sulph. sumb. tarax. teucr. thuj. valer. verat-v. verat. zing.

ABDOMEN - PAIN - flatus; passing - amel. all-c. aloe am-c. arn. bism. Calc-p. Carb-v. cham. Cimx. coloc. Con. corn. crot-t. dulc. ferr. Graph. grat. Guaj. Iris jatr-c. kali-n. Lyc. mag-c. merc-c. NAT-AR. nat-m. Nat-s. nux-m. ox-ac. phyt. plb. Psor. Rumx. Sep. sil. spong. sulph. Tarent. til.

ABDOMEN - PAIN – Intestines Dios. lacer. tab. thal-met.

ABDOMEN - PAIN – Sides acon. agar. all-c. Aloe alum. ant-t. ars. asar. bell. **Borx.** brom. bry. cadm-s. calc. canth. carb-an. carb-v. castm. **Cham.** chin. coloc. com. con. cupr. elaps eup-pur. eupi. ferr-ar. ferr. fl-ac. graph. grat. haem. hep. ign. iris kali-n. kalm. lach. laur. lith-c. lyc. m-ambo. mag-c. manc. med. mur-ac. murx. naja nat-c. nat-m. **Nat-s. Nux-v.** par. phos. plb. prun. rhus-t. rhus-v. sars. sec. seneg. sep. sphing. sul-ac. sulph. tarent. thuj. valer. zinc.

ABDOMEN - PAIN - stool - after - amel. agar. aloe alum. apoc. ars. bapt. borx. bov. bry. **Calc-p. Carb-v.** chel. chinin-s. cimic. cinnb. coc-c. **COLCH. COLOC.** dig. dios. dirc. ferr. **GAMB.** gels. grat. helon. mag-c. nat-ar. nat-c. **Nat-s. NUX-V.** phos. podo. **Rheum Rhus-t.** senec. sil. sulph. thuj. trom. verat. zinc.

ABDOMEN – RETRACTION acon. agar. **Alum.** am-c. **Apis** arn. ars. **Bar-c.** bell. borx. **Bry.** calc-p. camph. canth. **Carb-ac. Carb-v.** caust. **Cocc.** colch. **Con.** crot-t. **Cupr.** dig. **Dros.** elat. euph. gamb. **HYDR. Iod.** iodof. jatr-c. kali-bi. kali-br. kali-c. laur. led. lob. lyc. merc-c. merc. mez. mosch. mur-ac. nat-c. **Nat-m.** nat-n. **Nux-v.** op. paeon. phos. plat. **Plb-act.** plb-chr. **PLB.** podo. ptel. puls. quas. sec. sil. staph. stram. sul-ac. **Sulph. Tab.** ter. thal-s. thuj. valer. **Verat. Zinc.**

ABDOMEN - RUMBLING - colitis begins; for several days before puls.

CHILL - DIARRHEA - during - mucous colitis cop.

EXTREMITIES - PAIN - Joints - wandering, shifting pain aesc. anag. **Ant-t.** arb. **Ars. AUR.** berb. **Calc-p. Camph.** cedr. chel. **Cinnb. Coca Cocc. Colch.** ferr-p. form. hell. **Hyper. Iris KALI-BI. Kali-s. Kalm.** lac-ac.

LAC-C. Lach. Mang. Merc-c. nat-ar. nat-s. nux-m. phyt. PULS. Rhod. sabin. tub.

EXTREMITIES - PAIN – Joints abrot. Acon-c. acon. aesc. agar-ph. agar. all-c. alum-p. alum-sil. Alum. alumn. am-c. am-m. am-p. anh. Apis Apoc-a. Apoc. aran. ARG-MET. arg-n. arist-cl. ARN. Ars-i. ars-s-f. Ars. arthr-u. asaf. asc-t. aster. aur-ar. aur-i. aur-s. aur. bar-c. bar-i. bar-m. bell-p. Bell. benz-ac. berb. Bol-la. BRY. cadm-met. caj. Calc-f. calc-i. CALC-P. calc-s. Calc. cann-i. Caps. carb-ac. carb-an. Carbn-s. casc. Caust. cedr. Cham. chel. Chin. chinin-ar. cimic. Cimx. Cinnb. cist. Cit-v. Cocc. Coch. Colch. Coloc. com. con. convo-s. cop. cot. croc. crot-t. cycl. daph. dig. dios. dros. Dulc. euon. eys. Ferr-ar. ferr-i. Ferr-p. Ferr. gels. Guaj. hell. hippoz. hist. hydr. hydrc. ign. Iod. ip. iris jac-c. jatr-c. Kali-bi. Kali-c. kali-n. kali-p. kali-s. kali-sil. Kalm. kreos. Lac-ac. Lac-c. lappa LED. Lyc. lyss. mand. mang-act. Mang. med. Merc. mez. morph. Nat-ar. nat-m. Nat-s. nit-ac. NUX-V. ol-an. par. penic. petr. Ph-ac. Phos. Phyt. PLB. psil. PULS. rad-br. Ran-b. ran-s. raph. Rheum Rhod. RHUS-T. rumx. Ruta sabad. Sabin. sal-ac. Sang. sel. senec. Sil. sol-ni. sol-t-ae. Staph. sul-ac. Sulph. syph. tarent. ter. thuj. tub-r. tub. verat-v. zinc.

EYE - INFLAMMATION - Episclera and sclera acon. bell. bry. kali-i. merc-c. rhus-t. ter. THUJ.

EYE - INFLAMMATION – Uvea toxo-g.

GENERALS - ANEMIA - disease; from exhausting acet-ac. alst. Calc-p. Chin. chinin-s. Ferr. helon. kali-c. Nat-m. Ph-ac. Phos. sec.

GENERALS - ANEMIA - hemorrhage; after Arg-o. Ars. Calc. Carb-v. CHIN. crot-h. FERR. Helon. hydr. ign. Lach. nat-br. Nat-m. Nux-v. Ph-ac. Phos. sabin. staph. Sulph.

GENERALS - ANEMIA - nutritional imbalance; from alet. alum. Calc-p. ferr. helon. nux-v.

GENERALS - EMACIATION - nutrition; gradual emaciation from impaired ars.

GENERALS – MALNUTRITION abrot. alf. aln. bac. BAR-C. berb-a. borx. Calc-hp. CALC-P. Calc. caust. crot-h. glyc. Graph. Ichth. iod. kreos. Lac-c. lac-d. lec. Lyc. med. NAT-M. ol-j. pin-s. sabal sacch. sanic. sil. thyr.

KIDNEYS – STONES act-sp. alum. am-c. am-m. ambr. Ant-c. apoc. Arg-n. arn. baros. bell-p. bell. BENZ-AC. Berb. cact. cal-ren. CALC. Cann-xyz. Canth. cham. chin. chinin-s. Chlf. cimic. coc-c. coloc. Dios. epig. equis-h. erig. ery-a. eup-pur. fab. frag. gali. guat. hed. hedeo. hep. hydrang. ipom-p. kali-bi. kali-c. kali-i. lach. lipp. LITH-C. LYC. mag-p. med. mill. nat-m. Nit-ac. nux-m. nux-v. oci. onis. op. oxyd. PAREIR. Petr. Phos. pipe. polyg-h. rub-t. Ruta saroth. SARS. Sep. Sil. solid. Stigm. sulfa. sulph. Tab. ter. thlas. thuj. urt-u. uva vesi. Zinc.

MOUTH – APHTHAE acet-ac. achy-a. Aeth. agar. all-s. allox. alum-sil. alum. anac-oc. anan. Anis. ant-c. ant-t. apis aral. arg-met. arg-n. Ars-i. ars-s-f. ARS. Arum-t. asim. astac. aur-ar. aur-i. aur-m. aur-s. aur. BAPT. bell. Berb. BORX. brom. bry. cadm-met. calc-i. calc-sil. Calc. Camph. canth. caps. Carb-ac. Carb-an. Carb-v. carbn-s. caul. cean. cham. Chel.

Chin-b. chin. chinin-ar. chlor. cic. cinnb. clem. cocc. corn. cub. der. Dig. dulc. elaps eucal. Eup-a. ferr-s. Ferr. ferul. gamb. Hell. Hep. hippoz. hydr. Hydrin-m. Iod. Ip. Jug-c. Kali-ar. Kali-bi. Kali-br. Kali-c. KALI-CHL. kali-i. Kali-m. kali-s. kali-sil. Kreos. Lac-ac. lac-c. lac-d. Lach. Lyc. Mag-c. mand. med. MERC-C. Merc-cy. Merc-d. MERC. MUR-AC. Myric. Nat-ar. nat-c. nat-hchls. Nat-m. Nit-ac. nux-m. NUX-V. oci-sa. ox-ac. oxyg. petr. Phos. phyt. plan. Plb. psil. psor. ran-b. ran-s. Rhus-g. rhus-t. sal-ac. sanic. Sars. sec. Semp. sep. sil. sin-n. Staph. SUL-AC. sul-i. SULPH. tarent. ter. thuj. tub. vinc. zinc.

RECTUM - DIARRHEA - alternating with – constipation
Abrot. acet-ac. agar. ail. aloe alum. am-m. ANT-C. ant-t. anth. Arg-n. ars-i. ars-s-f. Ars. aur-ar. aur-i. aur-m-n. aur-s. Aur. bell. berb. Bry. but-ac. calc-chln. calc. Carb-ac. carbn-s. Card-m. Casc. CHEL. Cimic. cina Cob. coff. colch. Coll. Con. cop. cor-r. crot-h. Cupr. Dig. dios. ferr-cy. Ferr-i. Ferr. gamb. glycyr-g. gnaph. Graph. grat. guat. hell. Hep. hom-xyz. Hydr. Ign. Iod. kali-ar. kali-bi. Kali-c. Kali-n. kali-s. Lac-d. Lach. Lact. Lec. lil-t. Lyc. mag-s. Manc. Mang. merc. mez. nat-ar. nat-c. Nat-m. nat-p. Nat-s. NIT-AC. Nux-m. NUX-V. OP. Phos. Plb. PODO. polyg-h. psor. Ptel. Puls. rad-br. rhus-t. Ruta sang. saroth. sars. sep. Staph. stram. sul-i. Sulph. sumb. Tab. thymol. Tub. verat. vib. visc. zinc-p. zinc.

RECTUM - DIARRHEA - night - midnight - after - 1 h - 1-3 h asc-t.

RECTUM - DIARRHEA - night - midnight - after - 1 h - 1-4 h Psor.

RECTUM - DIARRHEA - night - midnight - after - 12 h; until ars. cist.

RECTUM - DIARRHEA - night - midnight - after - 2 h - 2-3 h Iris phos.

RECTUM - DIARRHEA - night - midnight - after - 2 h aran. Ars. cic. phos. rhus-v. tab.

RECTUM - DIARRHEA - night - midnight - after - 3 h - 3-11 h nat-m.

RECTUM - DIARRHEA - night - midnight - after - 3 h - 3-4 h aeth. Kali-c. lyc.

RECTUM - DIARRHEA - night - midnight - after - 3 h cimic. mag-c. nat-c. petr. phos. podo.

RECTUM - DIARRHEA - night - midnight - after - 4 h - 4-6 h All-c. phos.

RECTUM - DIARRHEA - night - midnight - after - 4 h - 4-7 h nuph.

RECTUM - DIARRHEA - night - midnight - after - 4 h fl-ac. form. mang. Petr. phos. PODO. Rhus-t. sec.

RECTUM - DIARRHEA - night - midnight - after - 5 h - 5-6 h Nuph.

RECTUM - DIARRHEA - night - midnight - after - 5 h Aloe alum-sil. carbn-s. Phos. podo. rumx. SULPH. syph. tub.

RECTUM - DIARRHEA - night - midnight – after all-c. aloe Arg-n. ars-s-f. ARS. arum-t. asc-t. bry. Chin. Chinin-ar. cic. cist. dros. FERR-AR. ferr-p. ferr. fl-ac. gamb. hipp. iris KALI-AR. kali-c. kali-s. lyc. manc.

merc-c. nat-ar. nat-m. Nux-v. rhus-t. sec. squil. staph. stront-c. SULPH. Verat.

RECTUM - DIARRHEA - night - midnight – before mag-c. nux-m. puls. rhus-t.

RECTUM - DIARRHEA – night abrot. acon. aeth. aloe anac. ang. ant-c. ant-t. ARG-N. Arn. ars-s-f. ARS. arum-t. asaf. asc-t. aur-ar. aur-m. aur-s. Aur. bar-c. bar-s. borx. bov. brom. Bry. caj. canth. Caps. carb-v. Carbn-s. Caust. cench. Cham. Chel. CHIN. CHININ-AR. Chinin-s. chlol. Cinnb. cist. colch. Con. Crot-t. cub. diosm. DULC. FERR-AR. ferr-p. Ferr. fl-ac. Gamb. Graph. Grat. hep. hipp. Hyos. ign. ip. IRIS jal. KALI-AR. Kali-bi. Kali-c. kali-p. kali-s. kali-sil. kreos. LACH. lith-c. lyss. Mag-c. mag-m. manc. merc-c. MERC. Mosch. NAT-AR. Nat-c. nat-m. Nat-p. NUX-M. petr. ph-ac. Phos. PODO. PSOR. PULS. Rheum Rhus-t. sang. sel. senec. Sep. Sil. stront-c. Stry. SUL-AC. SULPH. Tab. ther. Tub. verat. visc. zinc.

RECTUM - PAIN - colitis; during – tenesmus MERC-C.

STOOL - FORCIBLE, sudden, gushing Acal. acon. ail. aloe am-c. ant-c. Apis Apoc. aran. Arg-n. arn. Ars. aster. aur-fu. bar-c. bell. BRY. calc-f. calc-p. canth. cench. cic. cist. cob. cocc. Colch. coloc. Crot-h. CROT-T. Cupr. cycl. dig. dios. dirc. Dulc. ELAT. fago. Ferr. Gamb. graph. GRAT. Ign. Iod. ip. Iris jal. JATR-C. Kali-bi. kali-n. lac-c. lach. lyc. lycps-v. mag-c. Mag-m. mag-p. merc-sul. Merc. mez. naja NAT-C. NAT-M. Nat-s. nicc. nux-v. op. Ox-ac. Petr. Phos. pic-ac. plat. PODO. psor. puls. Ran-b. Raph. rheum rhod. rhus-t. rhus-v. rumx. sang. sars. SEC. seneg. Sep. sil. sulfonam. Sulph. tab. Thuj. trom. tub. VERAT. verb. viol-t. zinc.

STOOL - HARD - followed by - fluid stool agar. aloe alum. am-c. am-m. ang. arund. asaf. bar-c. borx. BOV. calc-f. calc-p. CALC. canth. carb-an. carbn-s. chin. coff. coloc. euph. graph. grat. ign. kali-bi. kali-n. lact. LYC. mag-c. mag-m. mosch. mur-ac. nat-c. Nat-m. nat-s. nux-m. nux-v. olnd. op. ph-ac. phos. plat. plb. rheum rhus-t. sars. sep. spig. spong. stann. staph. Sul-ac. sulph. tarent. zinc.

STOOL – MUCOUS acon. aesc. Aeth. agar. agra. allox. aloe alum. am-c. Am-m. ang. ant-c. ant-t. Apis ARG-N. arist-cl. Arn. ars-i. Ars. Asar. asc-t. aur-m-n. bac. Bapt. bar-c. Bell. Berb. Borx. Brom. Bry. cact. cadm-s. calc-act. Calc-p. calc. Canth. CAPS. Carb-ac. carb-an. Carb-v. carbn-s. castm. Caust. Cham. chap. Chel. Chin. cic. cimic. cina cinnb. Cocc. COLCH. COLL. Coloc. con. Cop. Corn. Crot-c. Crot-t. cupr. cycl. dig. dios. dirc. dros. Dulc. elat. euph. ferr-ar. ferr-i. ferr-p. ferr. gal-ac. GAMB. geo. Glycyr-g. GRAPH. grat. guaj. guat. ham. HELL. Hep. hydr. Hyos. ign. Iod. Ip. Kali-bi. Kali-c. Kali-chl. kali-i. kali-m. kali-n. kali-p. KALI-S. kali-sil. lach. laur. led. lil-t. lyc. lycps-v. m-aust. Mag-c. mag-m. mag-s. MERC-C. merc-d. MERC. Mur-ac. naja nat-ar. nat-c. nat-m. nat-p. Nat-s. nicc. Nit-ac. nux-m. NUX-V. ox-ac. oxyt. par. petr. Ph-ac. PHOS. Phyt. Plb. Podo. prun. Psor. PULS. raph. Rheum rhod. Rhus-t. ric. Ruta sabad. sabin. samb. Sec. sel. seneg. sep. Sil. solid. spig. Squil. Stann. Staph. stict. Sul-ac. SULPH. tab. ter. trom. tub. urt-u. vario. VERAT. viol-t.

STOOL – THIN abrom-a. acet-ac. Aeth. agar. agn. allox. Aloe alum-p. alum-sil. ALUM. ammc. anan. ang. ANT-C. ant-t. APOC. Aran. arg-n. Arn. ars-s-f. Ars. arum-t. ASAF. asar. asc-t. aster. aur-ar. aur-s. aur.

bapt. bar-m. **Bell. BENZ-AC.** bism. borx. **Bov.** brom. **Bry.** cadm-met. cain. calad. calc-p. calc-sil. **CALC.** camph. cann-xyz. canth. **Carb-ac.** carb-an. **Carb-v.** carbn-o. **CARBN-S.** cassia-s. castor-eq. **Caust. Cedr. Cham. Chel. Chin. Chinin-ar. Cic.** cist. **Clem. Cocc. Coff. COLCH. Coloc. Con.** cop. corn. cortiso. **CROT-T.** cupr. cycl. dig. dios. dros. dulc. epil. euph. ferr-p. ferr. **GAMB. GRAPH. Grat.** guaj. guat. hell. **Hep.** hip-ac. **Hydr.** hyos. ign. ind. ip. iris jal. **JATR-C. Kali-bi.** kali-c. kali-n. kali-s. **Lac-ac. Lach.** laur. lept. luf-op. **LYC.** m-aust. **Mag-c.** mag-m. mang-s. med. meph. merc-c. merc-i-f. **Merc.** mez. mim-p. **Mur-ac.** narc-ps. nat-ar. nat-c. nat-m. **Nat-p. NAT-S.** nicc. nit-ac. **Nuph. Nux-m. Nux-v.** oci-sa. **OLND. Op.** opun-s. osm. par. petr. **PH-AC. PHOS.** phyt. **PIC-AC.** plat. **PODO. Psor.** ptel. puls. pyrog. ran-s. rat. rheum rhod. **Rhus-t.** rhus-v. rumx. sabad. sabin. samb. sang. saroth. sec. sel. senec. **Sep. Sil.** sphing. **Spig. Spong. Squil.** stann. staph. stront-c. sulfonam. **SULPH.** tab. **Tarent.** tell. **THUJ. Trios.** trom. vario. **VERAT.** visc. yohim. zinc.

Homoeopathic Therapeutics for IBD and IBS

Homeopathy offers various remedies for gastrointestinal problems, focusing on individualized treatment based on specific symptoms and patient characteristics. Here are some commonly used homeopathic remedies for gastrointestinal issues:

Abies Nigra: Useful for a sensation of a lump or heavy weight in the stomach after eating, often with indigestion and bloating. It suits individuals who have a sedentary lifestyle.

Aconitum Napellus: Indicated for sudden onset of gastrointestinal symptoms, such as diarrhea or vomiting, often following exposure to cold or fright. It suits individuals who are anxious and restless.

Aethusa Cynapium: Used for violent vomiting and diarrhea in infants, particularly after consuming milk. It suits individuals who are exhausted, pale, and have a sunken appearance.

Allium Sativum: Indicated for digestive issues related to overeating, particularly of garlic or spicy foods, with bloating and gas. It suits individuals who are robust and prone to dietary indiscretions.

Aloe Socotrina: Indicated for diarrhea with a sudden urge and abdominal pain, especially in the morning or after eating. It suits individuals who are irritable and worse from heat.

Alumina: Indicated for severe constipation with a lack of urge to defecate and dry, hard stools. It suits individuals who are elderly or have a tendency toward sluggish bowel movements.

Anacardium Orientale: Indicated for indigestion and bloating with a sensation of a lump or plug in the stomach. It suits individuals who are irritable, feel worse with mental exertion, and have a tendency toward forgetfulness.

Antimonium Crudum: Useful for indigestion, nausea, and vomiting, particularly after overeating or consuming rich foods. It suits individuals who are irritable and dislike being touched.

Antimonium Tartaricum: Indicated for nausea, vomiting, and loose stools with a coated tongue and a sensation of fatigue. It suits individuals who feel worse with warmth and better with fresh air.

Argentum Nitricum: Beneficial for anxiety-related digestive issues, such as diarrhea before important events. It suits individuals who are hurried, anxious, and crave sweets.

Arsenicum Album: Useful for food poisoning, gastroenteritis, and burning stomach pain, especially when symptoms are accompanied by restlessness, anxiety, and a desire for frequent sips of water.

Aurum Metallicum: Indicated for digestive problems associated with a feeling of hopelessness or deep-seated grief, such as indigestion and stomach ulcers. It suits individuals who are melancholic and worse at night.

Baryta Carbonica: Effective for chronic constipation with hard, dry stools, often in elderly individuals or those with developmental delays. It suits individuals who are shy, timid, and slow in mental or physical development.

Belladonna: Effective for acute gastroenteritis with sudden, intense abdominal pain and inflammation. It suits individuals who are sensitive to light and noise, with flushed faces and dilated pupils.

Berberis Vulgaris: Indicated for liver and gallbladder issues, such as gallstones or biliary colic, with sharp, radiating pain. It suits individuals who experience discomfort that extends to the back and feel worse with movement.

Bismuthum Subnitricum: Effective for vomiting, especially when accompanied by a sensation of coldness in the stomach. It suits individuals who feel better with warmth and after vomiting.

Bryonia: Effective for constipation with dry, hard stools and a sensation of heaviness in the abdomen. It suits irritable individuals who prefer to stay still.

Calcarea Carbonica: Effective for sluggish digestion, bloating, and constipation, especially in individuals with a tendency to gain weight easily and who are sensitive to cold and damp.

Capsicum Annuum: Effective for gastrointestinal issues with burning pain and a sense of heat in the stomach, often accompanied by a craving for stimulants like coffee or alcohol.

Carbo Vegetabilis: Used for bloating, belching, and flatulence, especially when symptoms are aggravated by lying down. It suits individuals who feel weak and prefer fresh air.

Carduus Marianus: Useful for liver-related digestive disturbances, including jaundice and gallbladder inflammation, with a sensation of fullness and pain in the right upper abdomen. It suits individuals who feel better with rest and warmth.

Caulophyllum: Useful for gastrointestinal spasms and colic, particularly in women with menstrual irregularities. It suits individuals who experience digestive disturbances in conjunction with their menstrual cycle.

Causticum: Useful for chronic indigestion and heartburn, especially when accompanied by a sensation of burning and rawness. It suits individuals who feel worse with dry, cold weather and better in damp conditions.

Chamomilla: Effective for abdominal pain and colic in infants and children, particularly when associated with irritability and restlessness. It suits individuals who are oversensitive to pain.

Chelidonium Majus: Effective for liver and gallbladder conditions, including jaundice, with right-sided abdominal pain and yellow discoloration of the skin. It suits individuals who feel better with warm drinks and lying on the left side.

Chionanthus Virginica: Indicated for liver and pancreatic disorders, including jaundice and gallstones, with severe pain and digestive upset. It suits individuals who feel worse after eating and better with rest.

Cinchona Officinalis (China): Beneficial for bloating and gas after loss of fluids, such as from diarrhea or excessive sweating. It suits individuals who feel better with pressure on the abdomen and worse with light touch.

Cocculus Indicus: Beneficial for nausea and vomiting, particularly motion sickness or vertigo-related digestive disturbances. It suits individuals who feel worse from loss of sleep and mental exertion.

Colchicum Autumnale: Useful for digestive issues with distension and pain, particularly after consuming spoiled or heavy foods, with nausea from the smell of food. It suits individuals who are sensitive and feel worse with movement.

Colocynthis: Recommended for abdominal cramps and colic, relieved by bending double or applying pressure. It suits individuals experiencing anger and indignation.

Croton Tiglium: Indicated for sudden, explosive diarrhea with severe cramping pain, often triggered by drinking water or eating. It suits individuals who feel worse with the least amount of food or drink.

Digitalis Purpurea: Effective for nausea and vomiting with a slow, irregular pulse, often related to heart issues. It suits individuals who feel worse after drinking and better with rest.

Dioscorea: Useful for severe, cramping abdominal pain that is relieved by stretching backward. It suits individuals who experience pain that radiates to other parts of the body.

Euphorbia Corollata: Indicated for severe vomiting and diarrhea, often with cramps and cold extremities. It suits individuals who experience rapid onset of symptoms and feel better with warmth.

Ferrum Metallicum: Beneficial for digestive issues with weakness and anemia, often accompanied by alternating diarrhea and constipation. It suits individuals who feel better with gentle movement and worse with rest.

Graphites: Beneficial for chronic constipation with large, difficult stools and anal fissures. It suits individuals who are overweight and have a history of skin issues.

Gratiola Officinalis: Beneficial for chronic diarrhea with watery, frothy stools and a sensation of emptiness in the stomach. It suits individuals who feel worse after drinking cold water and better with warmth.

Hepar Sulphuris: Indicated for sharp, splinter-like pain in the stomach and sensitive digestion. It suits individuals who are sensitive to cold and feel worse with cold foods and drinks.

Hydrastis Canadensis: Indicated for chronic constipation with a sensation of incomplete evacuation and thick, sticky mucus in the stools. It suits individuals who are weak and have a tendency to mucous membrane issues.

Ignatia Amara: Indicated for gastrointestinal symptoms related to grief or emotional stress, such as indigestion and spasmodic pain. It suits individuals who are sensitive, prone to mood swings, and feel better with deep breathing.

Ipecacuanha: Useful for persistent nausea and vomiting, often without relief, especially when accompanied by clean tongue and excessive salivation. It suits individuals who feel worse with warm, stuffy rooms and better in fresh air.

Iris Versicolor: Effective for acid reflux, heartburn, and burning stomach pain that radiates to other parts of the abdomen. It suits individuals with a history of migraines.

Kali Bichromicum: Indicated for gastritis and peptic ulcers with a sensation of heaviness in the stomach. It suits individuals who experience symptoms in a periodic manner and feel worse with cold weather.

Kali Carbonicum: Indicated for bloating, gas, and a sensation of fullness after eating, especially when accompanied by back pain. It suits individuals who are conservative, rigid, and feel better with firm support.

Leptandra Virginica: Effective for liver and gallbladder issues with dark, tarry stools and a bitter taste in the mouth. It suits individuals who feel worse with movement and better with rest.

Lilium Tigrinum: Effective for gastrointestinal symptoms related to stress or emotional turmoil, such as indigestion and a sensation of pressure in the stomach. It suits individuals who are anxious and feel better with distraction.

Lycopodium: Helpful for bloating, gas, and constipation, often with a sensation of fullness after eating small amounts. It is suited for those who are apprehensive and lack self-confidence.

Magnesia Phosphorica: Used for abdominal cramps and colic, relieved by warmth and pressure. It suits individuals who experience spasmodic pain and feel better with warm applications.

Mercurius Corrosivus: Indicated for severe diarrhea with mucus and blood, often accompanied by tenesmus (a sensation of incomplete evacuation). It suits individuals who feel worse at night and better with warmth.

Mercurius Solubilis: Useful for diarrhea with a strong urge and tenesmus (a feeling of incomplete evacuation). It suits individuals who are sensitive to temperature changes and have offensive-smelling stools.

Momordica Balsamina: Beneficial for colicky abdominal pain and diarrhea, particularly in children. It suits individuals who experience sudden, sharp pain and feel better with pressure on the abdomen.

Natrium Phosphoricum: Used for acid reflux and sour stomach with a yellow-coated tongue. It suits individuals who have acidity issues and crave fried foods.

Natrium Sulphuricum: Useful for chronic diarrhea, especially in the morning, and digestive issues worsened by damp weather. It suits individuals who feel better in dry climates and worse in damp or humid conditions.

Natrum Muriaticum: Used for chronic constipation, heartburn, and bloating, especially when symptoms are worse after eating bread or salty foods. It suits individuals who are reserved and sensitive.

Nux Moschata: Useful for digestive issues with bloating and dry mouth, often accompanied by sleepiness and confusion. It suits individuals who feel worse with cold and better with warmth.

Nux Vomica: Effective for indigestion, nausea, vomiting, and constipation, particularly after overeating or excessive consumption of alcohol or stimulants. It suits irritable and impatient individuals.

Opium: Indicated for constipation with dry, hard, black stools and a lack of urge to pass stool. It suits individuals who are drowsy, lethargic, and feel worse with inactivity.

Phosphorus: Effective for gastritis, burning stomach pain, and vomiting. It suits individuals who are anxious, thirsty for cold drinks, and often crave salty or spicy foods.

Platina: Effective for constipation with hard, dry stools and a sensation of constriction in the abdomen. It suits individuals who feel better with movement and worse with rest.

Plumbum Metallicum: Beneficial for severe constipation with hard, knotty stools and abdominal pain. It suits individuals who have a history of neurological symptoms and feel better with firm pressure.

Podophyllum Peltatum: Effective for profuse, watery diarrhea with a sudden urge and gurgling in the abdomen, especially in the morning. It suits individuals who experience weakness and are worse with movement.

Psorinum: Useful for chronic digestive issues with extreme sensitivity to cold and a tendency to feel better in warm environments. It suits individuals who have a history of poor health and chronic conditions.

Pulsatilla: Indicated for indigestion, bloating, and diarrhea, particularly when symptoms vary and are worse after consuming rich, fatty foods. It suits individuals who are gentle, emotional, and seek comfort.

Raphanus: Used for severe gas and bloating that is not relieved by passing gas. It suits individuals who have a distended abdomen and feel worse after eating.

Rhus Toxicodendron: Beneficial for gastrointestinal symptoms associated with food poisoning, such as nausea, vomiting, and diarrhea, especially when accompanied by restlessness and aching in the body.

Ruta Graveolens: Beneficial for digestive problems with a sensation of pressure and heaviness in the stomach, often worsened by overexertion or strain. It suits individuals who feel better with lying down and warmth.

Sanguinaria Canadensis: Indicated for digestive issues with burning pain in the stomach and esophagus, often accompanied by headache. It suits individuals who feel better with sleep and worse in the afternoon.

Sarsaparilla: Indicated for digestive issues with colicky pain and a sensation of pressure in the abdomen, often related to urinary problems. It suits individuals who feel better with movement and worse with rest.

Sepia: Useful for digestive disturbances related to hormonal imbalances, such as nausea and constipation during pregnancy, with a sensation of heaviness. It suits individuals who feel better with vigorous exercise and worse with rest.

Silicea: Used for chronic digestive issues with bloating and constipation, especially when stools are difficult to pass. It suits individuals who are chilly, weak, and have a history of poor wound healing.

Spigelia Anthelmia: Effective for colicky pain in the abdomen with a sensation of twisting, often radiating to other parts of the body. It suits individuals who feel worse with movement and better with rest.

Stannum Metallicum: Indicated for digestive issues with a sensation of weakness and emptiness in the stomach, often with a sweet taste in the mouth. It suits individuals who feel better with warmth and worse with cold.

Staphysagria: Effective for gastrointestinal issues following suppressed anger or emotional stress, such as indigestion and colic. It suits individuals who are sensitive and prone to suppressed emotions.

Sulphur: Used for chronic constipation with hard, knotty stools, and a burning sensation in the rectum. It suits individuals who have a tendency towards skin issues and feel worse with heat.

Syphillnum: Beneficial for chronic digestive issues with severe constipation and a sensation of dryness in the mouth. It suits individuals who feel worse at night and better with movement.

Tabacum: Beneficial for severe nausea and vomiting, especially related to motion sickness or vertigo, with a sensation of sinking in the stomach. It suits individuals who feel worse with movement and better in fresh air.

Tarantula Hispanica: Beneficial for nervous digestive disturbances with intense restlessness and a need to keep moving. It suits individuals who are extremely irritable and feel better with music.

Taraxacum Officinale: Useful for liver and digestive disturbances, including indigestion and constipation, with a bitter taste in the mouth. It suits individuals who experience discomfort after eating fatty foods.

Urtica Urens: Effective for indigestion and bloating, particularly related to shellfish or rich foods, with a sensation of fullness. It suits individuals who feel better with movement and worse with inactivity.

Veratrum Album: Effective for severe diarrhea and vomiting with cold sweat and extreme weakness. It suits individuals who are cold, thirsty for ice-cold drinks, and feel worse with exertion.

Veratrum Viride: Indicated for gastroenteritis with intense vomiting and diarrhea, often with cold sweat and extreme weakness. It suits individuals who feel worse with motion and better with warmth.

Zingiber: Effective for indigestion, flatulence, and diarrhea, especially when symptoms are triggered by dietary indiscretions. It suits individuals who crave warm food and drinks.

Homeopathic remedies must be selected based on the individual's specific symptoms and overall constitution to achieve the best results. This personalized approach is central to homeopathy, as it considers the unique physical, emotional, and psychological aspects of each person.

Consulting a qualified homeopath is essential for several reasons:

1. **Accurate Diagnosis**: A professional homeopath can conduct a thorough assessment of your symptoms, medical history, and lifestyle to accurately diagnose the underlying issues.
2. **Individualized Treatment**: Homeopathy focuses on treating the individual as a whole

rather than just addressing isolated symptoms. A trained homeopath will tailor the treatment to your specific needs, ensuring that the remedy aligns with your overall health and constitution.

3. **Appropriate Remedy Selection**: With a vast array of homeopathic remedies available, selecting the most appropriate one can be complex. A qualified homeopath has the expertise to choose the remedy that best matches your unique symptom profile.

4. **Correct Potency and Dosage**: The potency and dosage of homeopathic remedies are critical to their effectiveness. A professional homeopath can determine the right potency and frequency of administration to maximize therapeutic benefits while minimizing any potential side effects.

5. **Monitoring and Adjustments**: Homeopathic treatment often requires ongoing monitoring and adjustments. A homeopath can track your progress, make necessary changes to the treatment plan, and address any new or evolving symptoms.

6. **Holistic Approach**: Homeopaths consider all aspects of your well-being, including mental, emotional, and physical health. This holistic approach ensures that the treatment addresses the root cause of your condition rather than just alleviating symptoms.

In summary, consulting a qualified homeopath is crucial for effective and personalized treatment. They will help identify the most suitable remedy, determine the correct potency and dosage, and provide ongoing support to ensure optimal health outcomes. This individualized care is the cornerstone of homeopathic practice, emphasizing the importance of treating the person as a whole.

Bibliography

Chapter 134. Systemic Autoinflammatory Diseases > Early-Onset Inflammatory Bowel Disease (IBD) Fitzpatrick's Dermatology in General Medicine, 8e ... Early-Onset Inflammatory Bowel Disease (IBD) at a Glance Very rare autosomal recessive disorder, early onset IBD (OMIM #613148). Mutations in IL10RA , on chromosome 11q23 or on IL10RB, on chromosome 21q22, encoding the IL-10 receptor Cutaneous features can include early onset...

Chapter 65. Inflammatory Bowel Disease The Color Atlas of Family Medicine, 2e

Common Large Intestinal Disorders > Colon Cancer in IBD Hazzard's Geriatric Medicine and Gerontology, 7e ... The risk of colon cancer in patients with long-standing IBD is a significant complication of the disease. Colon cancer rates generally are higher in patients with UC than those with Crohn disease; it appears to be the degree and extent of ongoing inflammation in the colon that confers...

Drugs Used in Gastrointestinal Disorders > G. Drugs Used in Inflammatory Bowel Disease (IBD) Katzung & Trevor's Pharmacology: Examination & Board Review, 11e

Encyclopedia Homoeopathica

Gastrointestinal & Biliary Complications of Pregnancy > A. Course of IBD During Pregnancy and in the Postpartum Period CURRENT Diagnosis & Treatment: Gastroenterology, Hepatology, & Endoscopy, 3e ... A recent meta-analysis of 14 studies reports the effects of disease activity at conception on the course of IBD in 1300 pregnant UC patients and 590 pregnant CD patients. The risk of active disease during pregnancy was much higher if disease was active at conception compared to those in remission...

Inflammatory Bowel Disease > COMMENSAL MICROBIOTA AND IBD Harrison's Principles of Internal Medicine ... The endogenous commensal microbiota within the intestines plays a central role in the pathogenesis of IBD. Humans are born sterile and acquire their commensal microbiota initially from the mother during egress through the birth canal and subsequently from environmental sources. A stable...

Inflammatory Bowel Disease > Diagnostic Criteria for IBD Clinical Genomics: Practical Applications in Adult Patient Care ...-ANCA) have high sensitivity for IBD in combination compared to other causes of intestinal inflammation, but sensitivity varies for different ethnic groups (much lower, eg, in regions endemic for tuberculosis). ASCA shows high specificity for CD, and p-ANCA for UC, although patients with CD limited...

Inflammatory Bowel Disease Principles and Practice of Hospital Medicine, 2e

Inflammatory Bowel Disease: Immunologic Considerations & Therapeutic Implications CURRENT Diagnosis & Treatment: Gastroenterology, Hepatology, & Endoscopy, 3e

Inflammatory Bowel Disease: Medical Considerations CURRENT Diagnosis & Treatment: Gastroenterology, Hepatology, & Endoscopy, 3e

Inflammatory Bowel Disease: Surgical Considerations CURRENT Diagnosis & Treatment: Gastroenterology, Hepatology, & Endoscopy, 3e

Pharmacotherapy of Inflammatory Bowel Disease Goodman & Gilman's: The Pharmacological Basis of Therapeutics, 12e

 Radar 10

Weight Loss, Unintentional > Alternative Diagnosis: IBD Symptom to Diagnosis: An Evidence-Based Guide, 3e ... IBD (Crohn disease and ulcerative colitis) are complex diseases. Genetic factors and commensal bacterial factors play a role. They are found most commonly in patients of Jewish descent and among patients with a family history of IBD. Crohn disease is a transmural process that may affect...

Index